D1413187

ONE-MINUTE PRAYERS™
FOR YOUNG MEN

CLAYTON KING

HARVEST HOUSE PUBLISHERS
EUGENE, OREGON

Cover by Dugan Design Group, Bloomington, Minnesota

Cover photo © iStockphoto / Zocha_K

Clayton King is represented by attorney/agent Thomas J. Winters of
Winters, King & Associates, Inc., Tulsa, Oklahoma.

ONE-MINUTE PRAYERS is a series trademark of The Hawkins Children's LLC. Harvest House Publishers, Inc., is the exclusive licensee of
the trademark ONE-MINUTE PRAYERS.

ONE-MINUTE PRAYERS™ FOR YOUNG MEN
Copyright © 2013 by Clayton King
Published by Harvest House Publishers
Eugene, Oregon 97402
www.harvesthousepublishers.com

ISBN 978-0-7369-5690-1
ISBN 978-0-7369-5691-8 (eBook)

Printed in China

17 18 19 20 21 / RDS-JH / 10 9 8 7

To my father,
Joe King. He was the greatest
man I've ever known. He was a
humble Christian, faithful husband,
and good daddy. I miss him
every day and hope I can one day
become half the man he was.

Contents

What You'll Find in This Book 7

Starting Out.................................... 9

Waiting 19

Where Is God?............................... 23

Your Choices 29

Losing.. 43

Hiding 49

What You're Made For............................ 55

When You Talk............................... 71

God, Make Me… 75

God, Give Me… 87

Praying... 95

Giving.. 107

Truth, Not Feelings 119

Making Replacements........................... 129

Choosing 141

Big Secrets 153

Money and Stuff 163

In the Battle 173

Who Is Jesus to You?............................ 181

What You'll Find in This Book

They say men don't read books. I say that's ridiculous. Of course men read books! We're not dumb, or uneducated, or uninterested. But we are busy, at times we're preoccupied, and we're covered up with a ton of stuff to do most of the time.

So as a guy, I wrote this book for guys, guys like us.

Whether you're a rough, tough jock who likes tackle football and deer hunting, or a more creative, indoors kinda guy who prefers low-impact fun and watching the game instead of getting clobbered in the game, this book has something to say to you. I have some things to say to you.

For 25 years I've been preaching the gospel and teaching people how to follow Jesus. I'm still learning myself. Over those years I've developed a genuine, deep passion for helping young men mature into good men who love God, respect women, provide for their families, work hard, tell the truth, and live a life of integrity—and who take Jesus seriously. There is a time when the little boy decides he's ready to grow up. I want to help you in that transition.

These chapters are short and sweet. They're real and raw and to the point. They're filled with illustrations and stories guys can relate to. They will challenge and inspire and motivate and convict you (if I've done my job). I wrote every single word myself, with you in mind.

I tried to write in an order and sequence that I would have enjoyed and understood when I was a young man. Some chapters are more stand-alone, while others fit into groups where I tackle a theme, like hard work, submission, handling money, or making wise decisions. Every chapter has one big idea, a takeaway you can remember, and each chapter will take you a minute or two to read.

I have faith that you'll be changed for the better by this book, but not just because you read it. You will actually have to put these things into practice. I hope you love Jesus more and gain practical wisdom on becoming a man of God as you read these pages and pray these prayers.

STARTING OUT

How to Begin

If you're like me, you find it easy to start things you think are important. We follow through with things that we enjoy or that we need.

This book can actually be both joy and necessity. It can help you connect daily to something you need (a relationship with God), and it can be a special treat that you enjoy (a few moments away from the distractions of everyday life).

So what is the right way to begin a book like this? How do you avoid getting halfway through these pages and losing interest, adding this volume to the growing pile of half-read books by your bedside or in your tablet?

The answer is simple: Begin with the end in mind. Read a chapter a day (it will take less than three minutes) until you're done. Pray the prayers. Underline stuff. Make notes in the margins. No pressure. You will most likely hear God speak to you. And you may be surprised at what He says.

> *Heavenly Father, I want to begin a new time in my life where I get to know You better. Help me reach the goal of not just finishing this book, but of becoming more like You and loving You more.*

Does God Talk?

Before I became a Christian, my parents were watching a preacher on TV who said that God spoke to him in a real human voice. This caught my attention... until I heard what the guy said God had told him. It had to do with large amounts of money. I lost interest.

But that doesn't mean God can't speak to you. He does talk to us, but He uses various sources and various voices.

He speaks to us from the Bible. It's the bestseller of all time, and for good reason. It's God's way of communicating to us that He loves us.

He speaks to us through people, like your parents, your friends, or your pastor.

He talks to us in everyday circumstances that we often miss because we're preoccupied with other things.

And He will talk to you here in this book. The one catch is...you have to read it. Keep your mind and heart open. Be listening for His voice. Be ready to see and hear some things He wants to say to you...because if you're listening, you'll find out that He's talking. And He doesn't need a TV preacher, just a listener like you.

Jesus, I am listening for Your voice. Help me to hear You clearly, and when I hear You, help me to obey what You say. Train my ears to hear Your voice and my eyes to see Your face.

Small Steps

My dad was the best man I ever knew. He was strong, tender, loving, and firm. I miss him every single day. I preached his funeral on Father's Day in 2012. That was the day my earthly father met my heavenly Father.

My dad suffered several heart attacks and survived open heart surgery. I was totally surprised when just a few days after triple bypass, the doctors forced him out of the bed, onto his feet, and down the hall...walking.

I objected, certain his heart was too weak to walk. They explained that he must take small steps—to avoid blood clots, to increase blood flow, and to strengthen the muscles and tissue around his heart.

Do you see the spiritual connection to your heart? A few moments a day reading a Bible verse or a chapter here is enough to get you moving. Small steps make a big difference. It's the only way to move forward. And your heart will thank you for it.

Lord, today show me small steps of faith
and obedience I can take as I journey closer
to You. Strengthen my heart with every
step. Help me do what I can do, right now,
trusting You with things I can't control.

Just Pick a Spot

Most every Christian I know struggles with spending time with God on a daily basis. It's difficult to carve out time in our lives when there's so much already going on. We get overwhelmed at the thought of a "daily quiet time."

But I learned something from my wife that helped me connect with God. I dropped a giant jar of salsa in the kitchen and it exploded and covered the whole floor. It would take a week to clean up. I wanted to sell the house and move. But she said, "Just pick a spot and get started." Good advice for both domestic life and spiritual formation.

I wrote this book for young men like you because I know what it's like to be in your shoes. This is a good place to start getting serious about your faith.

Lord, show me the spot in my life where
You want me to start working. Give me the
patience to stick with it, even if it's a mess
and I don't think I can ever finish. Help me
celebrate the progress I make with Your help.

Ask for It

Do you feel weird asking God for things? I do, especially when I consider all He's already given me. But He never gets tired of blessing us with good gifts.

For my thirty-eighth birthday, an old friend asked me what I wanted. Flippantly, I said, "Box seats to a Dallas Cowboys game, the best steak in Texas, and my three best friends tagging along." Imagine my surprise when he told me to clear my calendar and inform my friends that we were heading to Texas!

Now imagine what God is capable of giving you! Don't hesitate to ask Him when you have a need.

Jesus, You gave Your life for me and I know
You love me. Give me the courage to ask
You when I have a need only You can meet.
Remind me that nothing is too hard for You
and that You delight in answering me when
I ask You for things only You can provide.

Ask Again

It's easy to become frustrated when we ask for help, only to be ignored or forgotten. Nothing angers me more than to be on hold with the power company or the credit-card company, with a simple question, and to have them accidentally hang up on me.

In that situation, if I want assistance, I have to call them back. I have to ask again. Eventually, I get the help I need.

Don't give up on God just because He doesn't answer your question or meet your request the first time you ask. He may be teaching you tenacity. Ask again. Call back. He is not ignoring you.

God, show me how to keep praying, even when I feel like You don't hear me. Help me overcome my frustration with how You handle things and trust Your wisdom in my situation. Help me to keep asking.

Ask Why You're Asking

Maybe the reason God's not answering your prayer is because you're praying for the wrong reason. Instead of giving up, ask yourself why you're praying that prayer in the first place. If God always said yes to your prayers, would you be the primary person to benefit? If so, you may be praying selfishly.

God weighs our motives. He knows everything we do and He knows why we do everything we do (and why we pray for certain things). And He sees every possible outcome of all the prayers we pray. Like a daddy refusing to buy his 17-year-old son a new Corvette he can't handle, God loves us too much to always say yes to all our requests. This truth can help you understand why God sometimes says *no*.

> *Today I want to be mindful of my desires.*
> *God, help me question the secret motivations*
> *of my heart. Shine Your light of conviction*
> *upon my selfish agendas. Teach me to ask for*
> *things that help others and bring You glory.*
> *Give me understanding when You say no.*

When *No* Is Good

None of us like to be turned down or told no. It means someone has refused to give us something we wanted. But God has our best interest in mind when He turns us down. It is for our own good.

When I was in high school, I begged God to let me marry a beautiful girl in my class. I just knew she was perfect for me. The harder I prayed, the more convinced I became that we were meant to be together.

But God said *no*. I was angry and confused until a few weeks later when she dropped out of school because of her secret addiction to drugs. It turns out that God's *no* was actually *good*.

God, give me the faith to believe that You always want what's best for me. Help me remember that You have the authority over every prayer I pray, and You can answer them according to Your wisdom. I'll take no *for an answer anytime.*

Not Yet

Timing is everything.

I learned this when I moved up from JV to varsity baseball. I had to anticipate the timing of my swing because the pitchers threw the ball so much faster in high school than middle school.

The same is true in your relationship with Jesus. You may think you're ready for something—a girlfriend, a job, a starting position on the team, or your own car. The desire for that thing isn't wrong, but the timing may not be right. Maybe you're not ready.

God may not be telling you *no*. He may just be saying *not yet*.

God, I trust Your timing even when I don't agree with Your decision. If I am not ready yet, I submit myself to Your plan and Your process to grow me up in my faith. Begin now, Lord, by showing me how to wait on You and Your perfect timing.

WAITING

Work While You Wait

always carry my iPad with me when I travel. I also have my Bible and my journal. I do this because I've learned that as I travel and fly, things happen that cause delays, like cancelled flights or bad weather. I have no control when the weather turns bad, and I have to wait.

I learned that if I have to wait, I might as well work while I wait. This principle applies to our Christian life. While we're waiting on God to answer our prayers or come through for us, we should also be working on our spiritual growth and maturity. Keep reading the Bible, keep praying, and keep obeying God, even while you're waiting.

Lord, teach me not to zone out during those times when I don't always see what You're up to. I want to work at being a man of God during those seasons. Remind me that I need to wait on You, but I can be working on my character while I wait.

Waiting Well

I don't know about you, but I'm not a very patient person. I really hate to wait.

I hate to wait at restaurants, in line at ball games—and I hate waiting on other people. However, if you live in this world, you're definitely going to have to learn to wait. The world doesn't revolve around your schedule.

We also have to wait on God...not because He's late, but because we are not ready. When He doesn't do things on our schedule, we have to wait. The key is not waiting, because we don't have a choice. The key is waiting *well*. It's having the right attitude during those times when we wait—not complaining, but asking God to prepare us and get us ready for what He wants to show us or teach us.

God, I'm not naturally patient. I get upset when things don't go my way. Convict me during my times of impatience. And when I am forced to wait on You, help me to wait well, with an attitude of patient submission to Your Holy Spirit.

Why Wait?

Why do we have to wait all the time, anyway? Life would be easier if we could save all that time, right? Well, maybe not.

We have to wait because everyone else who is in front of us wants the same thing we want, but they got there before we did, so they go first. When I see the table next to me get their food before I do at a restaurant, it's usually because they ordered before me.

So don't get discouraged if you see your friends growing spiritually or getting their prayers answered before you. Maybe they've been waiting longer than you have. Be encouraged that the longer you wait, the closer you get to seeing God move or having your prayer answered.

> *God, help me to remember that when I see*
> *You blessing other people, You will also bless*
> *me if I will keep following and obeying You. I*
> *know there's no guarantee of the kind of*
> *blessing You will send, but I believe that if I*
> *wait on You, You will come through for me.*

WHERE IS GOD?

All Alone

Whether you're shy or outgoing, an introvert or an extrovert, you probably don't like always being alone. Though it can be restful to get away from the crowd at times, I always eventually feel pulled back to people.

God made you that way. He designed you to have interaction and relationships with other people. We need companionship. When we feel like no one cares for us, we immediately feel isolated and alone. And this is a scary place. We want to be noticed. We need to be loved.

But you are never truly alone. God is always there for you, with you, and by your side. Even when you can't see Him or feel Him, He is still there. He watches over you, gives you His Spirit as a guide and companion, and loves you more than you know.

> God, I need You to stay with me. I don't want
> to live a day without You by my side. When I
> feel all alone, I ask You to speak to me, nudge
> me, and remind me that You're right there
> with me. Thank You for being there!

In the Shadows

When I feel abandoned and wonder if God has left me to fend for myself, I remember a story I read in high school about a Native American tribe and their ritual for young boys as they entered manhood.

At age 13, a boy embarked on an adventure that was steeped in mystery because the older men kept it a secret. The boy was blindfolded, set on a horse, and led a day's journey into the wilderness by his father. Then he walked several hours on foot until dusk. His father told him he had to spend a night alone in the forest to conquer his fears and become a brave warrior.

Every sound and rustle would cause him to panic. His imagination created wild animals and monsters out of every little sound. Yet when the sun began to cast faint light across the trees the next morning, he saw the silhouette of his father standing a few feet away. He never left his side. He was there the entire time, watching over his beloved son.

Father, help me remember that You are
always by my side, even when You are
in the shadows and I cannot see You.

Closer Than You Think

Is there anything more miserable than being far away from the people you love the most? Whether it's your parents or your girlfriend or best friend, you just want to see them and be close to them. It brings you a sense of comfort and peace.

The same is true with God. There's nothing worse than feeling like He's distant or that your sin has separated you from Him.

I was homesick during college once and hadn't seen my parents in a few months. I went to preach at a church one Sunday night, and when I stood up to speak I caught sight of my parents in the audience, smiling! They had been there for an hour waiting to surprise me. I'd had no idea.

God is closer than you think, and sometimes when you least expect it, He shows up unannounced and surprises you with an answer to prayer, a sense of peace, or an encouraging word.

Lord, help me keep my eyes open. Train me to look for You and to expect to see You in unexpected places. And surprise me as often as You like!

A Surprise Visit

Is there anything better than getting a surprise visit from someone you love at just the time when you needed it? The more you love that person, the more meaningful the surprise.

Before I was married to Charie, I led a backpacking trek into the Himalayas, but because of the nature of the trip, it had to be an all-guys trip. I didn't see my girlfriend for a month!

When we landed, much to my surprise, Charie met me at the gate. She had made signs welcoming me home, she had snacks, and she gave me a big hug as she told me she'd loved and missed me while I was gone.

We tend to feel guilty if we have spent time away from God, but I try to remember that story from the airport now whenever I've missed my time with God. I imagine Him embracing me and telling me how much He loves and misses me when we're apart. It may help you too to think of Him in this way.

*God, I feel guilty when I fail to pray or read
Your Word. I need to see You in a different light.
Remind me that You just want to be with me
and know me. Help me overcome the negative
feelings when I forget to spend time with You.*

YOUR CHOICES

Make the Space

My high-school football coach told me that playing offense was about "making space." It was my job as a lineman to block the defenders and make the space for the running backs to run the ball and gain yards.

I've applied this lesson to my spiritual life. When I get too busy or overwhelmed, it feels like the space is closing in around me and I don't have room or time to spend with God. So I have to create the space in my life that allows Him to move, giving me room and margin to listen to His voice and follow His lead. This means saying no to lots of cool things so I can say yes to the best thing—a real relationship with Him.

Block out the distractions and create the space that you need for intimacy with the Lord.

God, show me the things in my life that are taking up important space I could open up for You. Help me see how to "make the space" by blocking out anything and everything that would distract my attention from You. By Your grace, we will move forward together.

His Grace Is Your Power

Let's be honest—it's really hard to say no, especially to something you really, really want. Yet in order to live a godly life, you know that you are going to have to resist certain temptations and say no to all kinds of things! It can get really frustrating. And you will want to give up and give in when it gets hard.

How can you possibly say no to so many tempting options?

By learning to trust in the grace of God and knowing that He is better than sin. When you think about His *grace*, think of His power and His ability to give you the strength you need to reject all the lies and resist all the temptations this world throws at you. You can't win by yourself. It's His grace, His power, that gives you victory.

> *God, open my eyes to the reality of Your*
> *grace and how it can teach me to say no to*
> *this world and yes to You. Give me more*
> *of Your power to live a godly life today.*

Close the Gaps

I was a defensive end on my high-school football team. My job, like that of every other defender, was to stop the offense from moving the ball. We did this by closing the gaps they tried to create. When there were gaps in the defense, the other team would score and we would lose.

When there are gaps in your spiritual life, things that you don't want to be there can slip through those spaces into your life. Things like greed, anxiety, lust, fear, and anger will stop you dead in your tracks.

Close the gaps through prayer, confession, accountability, and reading God's Word.

Heavenly Father, I know there are gaps in my life where I allow bad influences to enter in. Sometimes I don't have the energy or the courage to defend my heart, and I allow those things to distract me. I ask You to show me where the gaps are, and together You and I will work hard to close the places that allow bad things to enter my life.

Showing Up

The first and most basic rule that my coach enforced on our football team was simple—you had to show up every day. I had to be at practice. I had to be at team meetings. I had to be in the weight room, and I had to watch game film. There were no excuses, except maybe the flu. And I even played with the flu once.

The point is that you can't be good at something unless you show up, both physically and mentally. As a Christian, you can't grow or change or learn or be more like Jesus unless you "show up" every single day, putting Him first above all things. Be consistent in pursuing Him daily.

God, I confess that it is hard for me to pursue You every day. There are so many other things that fight for my attention. So when I am tempted to skip a day in prayer or in Your Word, remind me of what I miss out on when I miss a day with You. Help me to put aside other things so that I can put You first.

Find the Time

Life can get pretty busy. There are always things that need to be done. Homework, friends, chores, research papers, deadlines. During my senior year in high school, I was preparing for finals and I remember thinking, *I can't wait till I graduate and I can finally slow down!* Little did I know! I didn't realize how busy college life would be.

If you always wait for free time to "fall in your lap" before you connect with God in prayer, you will be waiting forever. You must grab the time. Find a few moments throughout the day to talk to God about your life. Start with 60 seconds of prayer between classes.

God, help me search for small nuggets of time every day that I would normally waste on meaningless things, and help me use those moments to talk to You in prayer. Help me remember that if I am looking for time, I will find the time.

On Display

You may be shy and introverted, or you may be outgoing and extroverted. Some people hate the spotlight. Some people love being the center of attention. Regardless of your personality, if you're a Christian, you represent the gospel of Jesus Christ to everyone in your life—the people in your family, at your school, on your teams, and at work. Even when you don't know it, you're on display.

Remember that the way you live, including how you talk, the way you treat others, and how you react to people, shows the people around you what Jesus is like. You are His representative. Your life puts Him on display.

Jesus, I want to represent You accurately and
correctly. I don't want to be a fake or a phony. Fill
me with Your Spirit and give me Your power
to be patient, kind, loving, compassionate,
and forgiving. Remind me that people are
looking at me and they are seeing You.

Set Apart

The word "holy" is most often used in an expletive, and it is most often understood to be a heavy religious word that creates visions of angels and smoke and altars like those in the book of Revelation. But it actually means "set apart."

Begin to think of yourself as holy—not super-spiritual or better than all your friends, but as a young man whom God has set apart for a specific purpose in life. Like your grandma's fine china, which is set apart for special occasions, or a wedding dress that has a specific use, or a star athlete like Michael Jordan or Peyton Manning, you have been set apart by God to show the world what a Christian really looks like.

Jesus, I feel intimidated when I think that You have a special assignment for me. I admit that I don't feel worthy or capable of being set apart as a witness. But I believe that You can use me, and I want You to use me. I receive Your power to enable me to be a testimony to others of who You really are.

Actions and Words

When I was 17, I flew on a plane for the first time—to Dallas, Texas, for a youth conference. I'd never stayed at a nice hotel before. I was so excited to ride the glass elevators up and down 30 floors! As I was acting hyper and having fun, some people on the elevator asked me if I was drunk.

Without thinking, I told them that not only was it illegal for me to drink at age 17, but that I was a Christian who was trying to follow Jesus Christ and by God's grace I intended to never get drunk.

Fifteen years later, I met one of the people who had been on the elevator. She told me that my words that day had made an impact on her heart and she'd given her life to Jesus as a result of my testimony.

You never know how God will use your words. Or your actions.

God, fill my mouth with Your words. Open my eyes to opportunities that I might otherwise never see. Prepare my mind and heart to be used for Your purposes. I submit myself completely to You.

Make a Difference

As a young man, you probably struggle at times feeling like people don't fully understand you or listen to you. I can relate. I used to get so frustrated when adults would blow me off or ignore me. I felt disrespected, so I would try harder and speak louder in an effort to make a point.

Then I heard a pastor say something profound, and it stuck with me: "It's better to make a difference than to make a point." That changed my perspective completely. Now instead of trying to make a point, I focus on making a difference.

The difference between the two is simple. Making a point is all about you. Making a difference is all about others and God.

God, I want to make a difference! I'm not interested in being heard or understood. Rescue me from the prison of my own selfish desires and set me free in the pursuit of Your purposes. I want to make an eternal difference for Your glory.

Leave a Mark

You're never too young to begin dreaming about the legacy you want to leave behind after you're dead.

That may sound morbid, but it's actually a cool idea that you should begin to consider. What kind of man do I want to become? What do I want people to say about me after I'm gone? What kind of mark do I want to leave on the world?

When I was on a field trip in middle school, I noticed a giant tree that had hundreds of names carved into it. All those people were leaving their mark in a small, insignificant way. I began to wonder if it was better to carve my name in a tree…or do the hard work of becoming a good man who could make the world a better place. I chose the latter. You should too.

Heavenly Father, help me begin dreaming of ways that I can leave my mark on this world. Purify my motives so my desire may be correct—to make a name for You and not for myself, so that others will know that You are alive and that You love them.

Built to Last

When I worked for my dad as a teenager in his motor shop, all the mechanics had their own toolboxes filled with tools—hammers, screwdrivers, wrenches, and sockets. I noticed that each one had the same name engraved somewhere on it, no matter what kind of tool it was: CRAFTSMAN.

This brand was guaranteed not to break, and if it ever did, you could get a brand-new replacement for free, no questions asked. It was a lifetime guarantee. They built their tools to last.

I want my faith in Jesus to last. To be more than an emotional high or a quick rush at a youth camp or concert. I want to be faithful for a lifetime to Jesus. And if I break, I know He will fix me, because He made me and He stands by what He makes.

Lord, give me a faith in You that can stand the test of time. I want to go the distance and follow You for life! Thank You for standing by me as You continue to make me into a man of God.

Get out of My Head!

Do you ever feel like the devil is attacking your thoughts? And do you get frustrated when you can't control the things you think about? My seven-year-old son has some good advice for you.

My wife had just told him not to climb on the kitchen cabinets. He disobeyed her, and when she caught him, he jumped down quickly and dropped a plate, breaking it. He was frustrated with himself and sat down at the table.

He told me that he prayed this prayer: "Lord, help me obey Mama. And devil, get out of my head! Quit trying to control me and make me do bad things that will get me in trouble."

Next time you're tempted, that may be the perfect prayer to pray.

Lord, when my mind is filled with temptations and bad thoughts, protect me from the enemy and his schemes to hurt me. Give me ears to hear You and a heart to obey You. I commit my mind and my thoughts to You.

LOSING

Sometimes You Lose

Most guys hate to lose. At anything. Checkers… football…hide and seek…you name it. But you can't always win. Sometimes you lose, and when you do, it's an opportunity for God to teach you about what really matters most.

I played baseball, basketball, and football beginning at age six, and boy, was I a sore loser! When we didn't win, I would get so angry I would cry. Then I would be embarrassed for crying, and that would make it even worse. This went on until I graduated high school.

After a tough loss, my dad said, "Son, sometimes you lose. And when you do, you become a better man by learning the lesson that there are more important things in life than winning games."

Jesus, I know that life is not a game. It's for real and it's forever. I want to live for more than temporary victories. I want to live for Your eternal kingdom. Teach me to be okay with losing, and to focus on developing a godly character as a man of God.

Losing Well

Okay. So we all know that we can't always win at everything. We will eventually lose…ball games, our temper, investments, and so on. The real question is not *if* we will lose, but *how* we will lose.

There's nothing more embarrassing than watching a parent throw a tantrum when their child's team loses a game. When that happens, we use them as an example for our sons on how to be a sore loser. Then we teach them how to lose well.

When my ten-year-old boy recently lost the county championship football game, he said, "It's okay. I don't like to lose, but there are more important things. Like my family, and the gospel, and being a good son and a good witness."

As it turns out, he teaches me as much as I teach him sometimes.

Lord, I know I can't always come out on top every time. So teach me how to lose well, how to exude Your patience when I don't always succeed, and how to show others what a Christian looks like when things don't always go their way.

Lose the Right Things

There are some things you never want to lose.

Your temper. Your car keys. Your wallet. You get the picture.

But are there some things you'd actually want to lose? I think there are.

It's good to lose your selfishness. Your insecurities. Your sense of entitlement. Your fear of stepping out in faith and trusting God. It's also good to lose your life—the old life that was filled with sin—so that God can replace it with a new life that's filled with joy and hope and peace.

God will replace the bad things you lose with better things. Trust Him. Lose the sin and get what you really need—a closer relationship with Jesus.

Jesus, I don't want anything in my life to
come between You and me. If there are
things I need to lose in order to gain a better
friendship with You, point them out to me
and give me the grace to walk away from all
of them, and to walk toward You in faith.

Lose Like Jesus

Whoever loses his life for Me and the gospel will find it. Jesus said this in Mark 8.

Did Jesus ever lose anything? It's a weird thing to think about, considering He was God even while He was a man on this earth. It seems like He would win every contest and every game show that ever existed. No one could ever beat Jesus.

But He didn't lose like that. The one thing He lost was His life. Yet no one defeated Him and caused Him to lose it. He laid it down as a sacrifice for our sins, giving us an example of how we should lay our lives down for Him and for each other. This is how we should lose just like Jesus—losing our selfish lives and finding real life in the process.

Jesus, teach me to lose like You. Show me opportunities to lay down my life for the sake of Your kingdom. I want to be like You. I take my eyes off of me and I place them completely on You. Remind me that losing is not bad as long as I am losing like You by giving up my life for something greater.

HIDING

Dark Secrets

Everyone has kept a secret at some point in their life. Little children are known for hiding things from their parents. My seven-year-old once confessed that he had a hidden stash of candy in his closet that he'd been taking from the kitchen. Secrets like that are fairly harmless, except for a little tooth decay.

There are other kinds of secrets we keep that have the power to do harm. I call them "dark secrets" because we tend to cover them up with darkness to hide them from God.

Do you have any secrets you are hiding in darkness for fear of being exposed? Addictions? Relationships? Thoughts? Bad habits? Lust?

There is only one way to break the power of a dark secret—confess it, own up to it, and bring it into the light. Begin by telling God honestly what you're hiding. This is the first step to freedom.

Heavenly Father, I confess that I sometimes hide things because I'm afraid. But You already know all my thoughts and actions, so I repent to You and receive Your love. Shine Your light upon my dark secrets and remind me that it's dumb to try to keep secrets from You.

Death Sentence

A dark secret can easily turn in to a death sentence. How does this happen? Slowly, over time, hiding a small sin allows it to grow into a major issue, and before you know it, you could be facing serious consequences.

I had a friend in high school who loved Jesus. He was one of my first mentors in the faith and had great influence on me. He was married with a family and had a great ministry, but he'd been hiding a dark secret for years—he was addicted to pornography. He confessed it to me, but never took the steps to get free from its power. It eventually cost him his marriage and his job, and it hurt his relationship with his kids.

He finally got serious about repentance, and later in life he saw God bring major restoration, but he paid a high price for many years. Don't let your dark secret turn into a death sentence. Start now by making daily confession a part of your prayer life.

God of mercy, I am not perfect. I have many flaws
and sins, but I know I can bring them before You
in prayer and You will listen to me and forgive me.
There is no death sentence when I belong to You.
Help me always come to You first when I fail or fall.

Conceal or Reveal?

It's funny to think we can ever hide anything from God. Seriously, do you really think that by trying to conceal your anger, insecurity, jealousy, or bitterness—whatever it is—you can actually fool the very Person who made you and knows everything about you?

The reason you have such a hard time revealing the "real you" to God is that you are afraid. You may be afraid of rejection, or of being embarrassed about a sin you've committed, or even that God will punish you for something you've said or thought.

So you have a choice—do you conceal, or do you reveal?

Always choose to reveal. God knows what you're hiding anyway. And if He were going to hurt you or make you pay, He would have already done it by now. He loves you! He forgives when we come to Him in humility. He is waiting to hear from you.

Lord, I'm often afraid to reveal my failures and sins to You because I'm afraid of losing Your love. Help me remember the sacrifice You made on my behalf when You gave Your Son for me. That is proof enough that You will not turn me away.

Hide-and-Seek

When I was a little boy, I clearly remember playing hide-and-seek with my parents, but not the kind of game where you actually hide in a closet or behind a door. This was the kind where I hid my face by covering it with both hands. I thought that when I covered my face, they couldn't see me.

Of course you and I both know how silly this is. My parents could see me the whole time. The same thing applies to us and God.

It's silly to think we can hide anything from Him. He's still right there, like my parents, watching me, loving me, waiting on me to take my hands away from my face.

Are you playing hide-and-seek with God? Stop covering your face! Open your eyes and see how much He loves and cares for you.

Father, Your Word tells me that You made me and You love me. I know it's silly to hide anything from You. Help me uncover my face, open my eyes, and see that You are right here with me, smiling at me like a loving Father who cares for His son. I never need to cover my face in shame because You have paid the price to take my shame away.

WHAT YOU'RE MADE FOR

Made to Love

When God made you, He created you in His own image. While I am not sure about all that this means, I do believe that we reflect many of His characteristics.

Maybe the greatest quality that we see in the Bible is love, and God Himself is the perfect definition and example of love. You were made in His image. He made you to express love to others.

You were made to love. It is in your spiritual genetics! When you show someone kindness, when you serve selflessly, you are being the man God made you to be by expressing His love to another person who needs it.

Father, teach me to love in a way that reflects Your perfect love to the world I live in. I want to start right where I live, with the people I come into contact with every day. I know I can't truly love them unless Your love fills my heart, so I pray in faith that You will give me an open heart and fill it with Your good gifts of forgiveness, mercy, and grace. Then help me to pour that same love out as freely as I have received it from You.

Made to Work

This may sound strange at first, but I bet that deep down in your heart, you actually love to work.

Few things feel as satisfying to a young man as putting in long hours, plenty of sweat, and the effort toward something hard, and then finishing well and feeling successful.

Think about how good it feels to study hard for a test and then find out you made an A! Or how about that feeling you get when you've spent countless hours practicing with your team and listening to your coach, and you pull out a victory in the game!

The reason you feel so good after an accomplishment is that God made you to work, and hard work pays off. Don't slack off. Don't complain. Work hard for the glory of God and rejoice when you see the blessings of your hard work.

Lord, help me find a new perspective on work, where I view it as an opportunity to honor You, advance Your kingdom, and build character. Thank You that I'm able to work for Your glory no matter what I endeavor to do.

Made to Gain

Jesus asked an important question in Mark 8. What do you really gain if you get everything in the world but lose your own soul?

Okay—let's tell the truth. Not many guys like to lose. Even when you were little, your parents and coaches had to teach you to be a good loser, right? It's because we are wired to gain and win, and losing hurts our competitive nature and our pride.

God made guys like this for a reason. He wants you to gain, but not like you think. Ultimately it doesn't matter if you win the game, win the gold, or win the girl. It only matters eternally if you win where it really counts—eternal life. If you gain everything the world has to offer but lose your soul, you've lost it all.

Jesus won the battle and the war for your soul. You gain because you belong to Him.

Jesus, I want to gain where it counts. I win in the end because You loved me enough to die for me and give me new life. That is the ultimate victory, and it's mine because of You.

Made to Provide

One of the cool things about my childhood was watching how my mom and dad worked together to take care of me and my brother. They were both hard workers who believed it was their duty to provide for their family.

I would ride to work with my dad in the mornings during summer break. My job was to sweep floors in his motor shop. I hated it. Until one morning he said to me, "Son, you're learning how to work at a young age. God wants you to provide for your own family one day. So take pride in your work and think about the future when you're sweeping floors."

You were made to provide, and work is how you do it. Don't miss the lessons you need to be learning right now when you have to do things you don't like.

Father, You provided a way of rescue for me.
You've provided me with life, health, and all
good things. I can never be a provider unless
I first learn to receive Your perfect provision
for my life. Thanks for taking care of me.

Made to Learn

I'm not sure what your favorite subjects in school are. I always struggled in math and science, so it was hard to pay attention and learn. But I loved history and literature, so it was a cinch to listen in those classes.

The challenge for young men like you is to learn how to learn. I know it sounds weird, but we really have to learn how to listen, pay attention, and apply the things that God teaches us in His Word and through our parents and leaders.

God gave you a brain that can retain information and apply it in real life situations. He made you to learn. Use that ability to make yourself a better child of His by paying attention to what He shows you and by doing what He tells you.

Heavenly Father, I want to learn all that I can possibly know about You, Your Word, and Your kingdom. I open my mind and my heart to Your wisdom. Fill me up as I learn to be more like You and to obey Your Word.

Made to Follow

My basketball coach had a phrase he would say to us when we weren't following the game plan during a game. He would call a time-out, gather us all by the bench, and say, "This is a team, and if you're going to play on my team, you'd better do what I say. Lead, follow, or get out of the way."

He was the leader and he called the shots. If you're a Christian, Jesus Christ calls the shots in your life—how you talk, how you treat others, how you spend your money, what you look at online, and how you handle relationships with girls. He is the boss, and He wants what's best for you.

Don't be foolish by trying to do things your own way. You will suffer if you do, I promise. You were created to follow good leaders, and Jesus is the best leader ever. He is more than a leader. He is Lord. Follow Him.

Jesus, I struggle with following Your Word and Your will sometimes. I forget that You're wiser and smarter than me. I trust that You want only what's best for me, so I am going to follow You no matter where You lead me.

Made to Lead

We are all made to follow Jesus, but are we all made to lead too?

You may not be a naturally gifted leader who becomes captain of the football team, student-body president, or the founder of a huge company one day. But as a guy, you are made to lead. Let me explain.

God wants you to lead others into a relationship with Christ. And you don't have to be super-confident or extremely outgoing to be this kind of leader. You just need to lead by example.

Lead others to see Jesus by showing them how a real Christian handles himself. In your speech, your actions, your grades, your temper, and your relationships, you are leading the people you are with every day closer to Jesus or further away from Jesus. You don't need to shout loudly or do anything epic. Just humbly and consistently portray a changed life, and you will be leading.

Jesus, I've never really thought of myself as a leader, but I see that You made me to lead other people to You by the example I set with my life. Help me always be mindful that others are watching me as I strive to live like a real Christian.

Made to Sacrifice

If you're like me, the word *sacrifice* causes you to cringe. Maybe it conjures up images of a lamb being laid on an altar in the Old Testament right before it's killed. Or maybe it makes you think of giving up all the modern conveniences you enjoy in order to move to a remote corner of the globe as a poor missionary.

I want you to see sacrifice in a different light. Think of it as a great honor—something you "get to do" instead of "have to do." Imagine God inviting you to join Him on His mission to redeem a broken world by giving up your rights to live life for yourself and instead living it for Him. It takes a strong man to lay down his rights for something greater than himself.

What a joy to sacrifice your own pursuits so you can join God on a more important mission—the adventure of bringing the lost and broken into His family!

God, I am willing to sacrifice whatever it takes so that I can be a part of Your greater work in this world. Whatever I have is Yours already. I give You absolute access to all that I am and all that I have.

Made to Build

When God gave Adam and Eve authority over the Garden of Eden, He did more than just tell them to name the animals. He gave them a mandate to build a family, a culture, and a way of life for the human race.

That same mandate from God lies in you. He's vested in you the ability to make good things for the benefit of the world you live in. I challenge you to begin dreaming now about ways you can change the world.

Maybe you will build a great company that will provide new products to help the poor. Maybe you will build a network of like-minded Christians who will rescue orphans from the streets of Bangkok or Port-au-Prince. Maybe you will build a strong church that prepares missionaries and sends out pastors to the far corners of the globe. Perhaps you will build a home filled with love.

Dream big and start building.

God, unleash my imagination today so I can dream about how You'll use me in days ahead. I want to dream big, crazy, audacious dreams that only You could make come true.

Made to Teach

A majority of classroom teachers in America are women, and there is certainly nothing wrong with that. But that doesn't mean that God can't use you to teach others just because you're a guy.

After I had been in ministry 15 years, a friend of mine asked me if I would personally disciple him. I said yes, even though I didn't really know how. So we started meeting regularly, and I simply taught him things I had learned as a Christian. It changed both of us, and he and his wife are now missionaries in the Himalayas for our ministry.

Begin looking at your circle of influence and see who God has placed near you. I bet there's a guy you know who would greatly benefit from your investment in his life. You could teach him! It's as simple as getting together and sharing lessons you've learned.

Lord, I pray that You would give me confidence to step out in faith and pursue opportunities to teach others. I also ask You to make it clear to me who I should begin to invest in as a brother in Christ. I am willing to share all that You've shown me.

Made to Celebrate

The opposite of criticism is celebration. No one wants to be friends with a critic, because you're always afraid they're sizing you up in order to tear you down. But people who know how to celebrate others' successes and blessings always have good friends—not to mention that they'll celebrate with you when God blesses your life!

God loves it when we celebrate with others. Just like I love to see my older son cheer on his little brother in a baseball game, our heavenly Father loves to see His kids cheering each other on.

Send a card or a text message or make a call. Pat your dad on the back or give your mom a big hug…and teach yourself to immediately rejoice with others when something good happens to them. It will make you a better man and a better friend.

Lord, make me aware of Your blessings to those around me so I can give You glory when You bless them. Reveal any jealousy in my heart, and forgive me for not rejoicing with others more often.

Made to Remember

The mind is a fascinating piece of machinery. I remember my first lie when I was 2, my first date when I was 15, and my first at-bat as a varsity baseball player. But when you need to remember something really important, like the answer to a question on your final exam, why can't you remember that?

The same thing happens to us spiritually. God has answered so many prayers for you, blessed you countless times, and taken care of you when you couldn't take care of yourself...so why is it so hard to remember His faithfulness when you're afraid?

God made you with the ability to remember. Exercise your memory by thanking God for all His goodness. Make a list. Keep a journal. Post it on Facebook. Tweet it to all your followers. The more you remember, the easier it will be to trust God when things are beyond your control and you need Him to come through for you.

God, I'm sorry for forgetting how You've helped
me and blessed me. I want to be a thankful man
of God. Refresh my memory when I begin to
fear and doubt Your ability and Your promises.

Made for Fun

The Greek philosopher Socrates is reported to have said, "I can tell more about a man by watching him at play for an hour than at work for a year." Certainly, God made guys to have fun!

Yet so many men miss out on true fun because they fail to see that the best fun is always honoring to God and free of regret. You don't have to be getting drunk, making out with a girl, or partying like a maniac to have a good time. So many of my friends and teammates would brag about how high they got or how many girls they hooked up with when we were in school. Yet years later when I bumped into many of them, they regretted those times, especially as they began having children.

Whether it's sports or a concert or hunting or fishing or movies or riding four-wheelers, God created you to enjoy all good things. He is happy when you find happiness in the things He created.

> *God, I hate feeling guilty and ashamed.*
> *Remind me that I can avoid feelings of*
> *condemnation when I choose to have fun*
> *in ways that honor You and don't hurt my*
> *reputation as Your son. Thanks for allowing*
> *me to have fun in this world You gave me!*

Made for Glory

If you watch college or professional sports, you'll notice how players celebrate after making a great play. After a good shot or a good catch or a big tackle they face the crowd and raise their hands, jump around, or taunt their opponent. They are basking in the glory of their accomplishment.

You are made for glory too—but not that kind, because that kind is not nearly good enough. The kind of glory you were made for is eternal, and it's not based on your making a good play in a game. It's based on Jesus taking your place on the cross and taking your sins away.

So the next time you hear a worship song or an old hymn, raise your hands! And realize you're not basking in the glory of your accomplishments, but in God's perfect accomplishment in saving you and giving you a new life.

Jesus, I want to live for Your glory alone. I have never done anything that can compare to all You've done, so I gladly give You all the credit and all the honor that You deserve.

WHEN YOU TALK

Speak Up

It can be tough to be a follower of Christ, especially in a culture that is growing increasingly intolerant of the Christian worldview. But it's essential that you speak up as a witness when you have the chance.

In the eleventh grade, our English class got into a big argument over the Bible, religion, and God. People kept making fun of "idiot Christians" who believed what they considered silly fairy tales, like the resurrection of Jesus or Moses' encounter with the burning bush. I knew that Jesus didn't need me to defend Him, but I needed to build up the courage in my heart to be His witness.

I was the only person willing to speak up that day, even though there were other Christians in the class. It didn't make me better than them. It simply showed me that God could give me courage in the middle of a scary scenario. He can give you the same courage, but you have to be willing to speak up.

Jesus, teach me when to be silent and when to speak up for You. Help me see the difference between trying to prove I am right and trying to be a witness for Your love.

Speak Out

Another area that you may struggle with is sharing your faith with someone who may not be a follower of Christ. It's not always possible to share the gospel with everyone you meet, but there are times when you know you should…and the temptation is to chicken out.

Don't chicken out. Speak out!

You don't have to be obnoxious or draw attention to yourself like a religious freak. You can simply take 30 seconds to talk to the person and tell them how Jesus changed your life when you began to follow Him. I've learned that the more I speak out to others about Jesus, the bolder I become and the more confidence I have in God's power to open people's hearts and minds to the gospel.

Speak out, and leave the results to God.

Jesus, in a world where so many people speak out about so many opinions, give me the courage to trust Your power when I know You want me to speak out about You. And when I am afraid to speak out, help me not to chicken out, but open my mouth in Your power.

Speak Last

The first summer that I ever worked as a camp counselor, I met one of my heroes—Josh McDowell, a famous writer and speaker. He spoke at the camp, and as I was talking to him after the service, I asked him for any advice he could give me.

He said, "When you're in a group of people and everyone is talking, always speak last, because the person who speaks last has the last word and usually sounds smarter, and people will remember what they said after they've forgotten everyone else."

Then he told me he was once in a meeting with President Ronald Reagan at the White House where this happened to him! After everyone gave their opinion, the president asked him what he thought. He spoke up. Then Reagan said, "I totally agree with you!"

*God, remind me that I don't have to always
speak first or loudest. Control my mind
and my mouth, and give me patience to
know when to speak, even if it's last.*

GOD, MAKE ME...

Make Me Teachable

One of the most important qualities you can begin to develop as a young man is learning to be teachable.

This goes beyond sitting up straight in class and taking good notes. It means having a hunger for knowledge. It means craving wisdom. It means desiring deep spiritual growth and maturity.

A teachable person seeks out older, wiser people and asks them questions. They keep a journal or a notebook, whether paper or electronic, with them all the time. They're constantly scribbling or typing notes, even when they're not in class. They set up meetings and meals with those they can learn from.

Begin now. Find ways to become a teachable man and you will never stop learning.

*Lord, teach me Your ways. Give me a hunger
to be taught about life, hard work, wise
decisions, and being a true disciple. Help me
seek out sources of knowledge and wisdom
and retain all that You teach me. Help me
avoid foolish people and foolish pursuits.*

Make Me Thirsty

During one of my summer breaks in college, I traveled to the Grand Canyon with my two best friends. We decided to hike the North Rim, but failed to plan correctly. On the 15-mile uphill hike back to the top, we ran out of water. It was 110 degrees. I actually thought I might die of dehydration.

The feeling of thirst was overwhelming, and I would've done anything for a drink of water. Have you ever prayed for God to give you that kind of thirst for His presence in your life? Have you ever thought about how quickly you would die without God, both spiritually and physically?

The best way to stay thirsty for God's presence is to practice being in His presence daily. The more you get to know Him, the more you will crave Him.

Create a thirst for Your presence in my heart,
God. May I find satisfaction and pleasure
only in knowing You and worshipping You
and You alone. I cannot live without You!

Make Me Humble

Of all the personal qualities of all the characters of the Bible that are recorded in Scripture, there is none quite like humility.

It's difficult to pursue humility in a culture that tells you to esteem and celebrate yourself. Biblical humility always deflects attention from you back to God—it is grounded in knowing your identity as a Christian. Humility flows from a proper understanding of how you deserved death and punishment, but instead were graciously given grace, life, and mercy through Jesus.

Pursuing humility is a lifelong journey, but it's worth the effort, for it always brings you back down to reality and reminds you just how dependent on God you really are for everything.

Jesus, make me humble. I want to follow Your example of humility, when You willingly died in my place. Create that same humility in me. Thank You for being patient with me when I fall back into pride and selfishness.

Make Me Faithful

Faithfulness is one of the most commonly mentioned qualities of God in Scripture. You should make it a goal in life that those who know you best use this word to describe you. There is nothing better you could strive for than to be a faithful follower of Jesus.

When my dad died, I had the honor of preaching his funeral. It was a powerful thing for me to be able to say that my dad was faithful to my mom every single day of their 50-year relationship. It was one of the last things he told me before he died.

Jesus was faithful to you when He died for you. He is still faithfully loving you today. So instead of trying to fit in, impress your friends, or stand out as the cool guy or the star athlete, pursue faithfulness to Him.

Jesus, I want to be faithful to You. I want to follow You all the days I live on this earth. I can't do it without Your strength and grace. I surrender my heart to You once again!

Make Me Bold

Sometimes we confuse being obnoxious with being bold. God doesn't want you to draw attention to yourself by screaming and shouting about your faith on a street corner or in a crowded mall. That defeats the purpose of being a witness for Jesus.

What He does want is for you to be willing and ready to tell your story of how God saved and rescued you. The best way to be bold is to practice it. And the best way to practice it is to be around other bold Christians. So find another guy who loves Jesus and hang out with him, watching how he talks to others about his faith. Then you go do the same.

When you are totally convinced that Jesus can change lives, it's easier to be bold, especially when you know how He changed you.

God, make me bold when I feel timid and give
me Your power when I feel afraid and weak.
This world needs to know Your saving power. I
want to be the one to tell them. Use me!

Make Me Trustworthy

Right now, think about all your friends—the ones you go to school with, play ball with, eat lunch with, and go to church with. Now, out of all those friends, how many of them would you hand your car keys to for the weekend?

Whoever those people are, the reason you would give one of them your car is because they've proven themselves to be someone that can handle responsibility. You would trust them with your car, or your checkbook, or your wallet.

That's a trustworthy person. God is looking for young men He can trust with His gospel, His kingdom, and the honor of representing His love to the world.

Don't you want to be a man He can call trustworthy? It starts with the next decision you make, and it grows from there.

God, I do want You to use my life for something bigger than me. I want You to look at me and see a trustworthy servant You can give big responsibility to. I ask You to prepare me for even greater things in the future by teaching me to be trustworthy in small things today.

Make Me Dependable

Being dependable is a lot like being trustworthy, but it means that you train yourself to follow through on small details and seemingly insignificant tasks that may not seem important at first glance.

A dependable person gets the job done. Are you the kind of guy that says you'll do something but then forgets about it, or only does the job halfway? Do you commit to things and then fail to finish? If so, you need to learn how to keep your word and be someone that others can depend on.

God doesn't need you, but He wants you. He wants to love you and He wants to use you. He depends on people just like you to show the world what a genuine Christian is. Being dependable is a priceless quality, so start in small ways today. It will lead to great opportunities in the future.

Lord, I want to be a dependable man of God.
Remind me that when I give my word, I need
to begin working immediately to keep my
word. And even if it seems like a small task,
there are no small tasks for a man of God who
wants greater opportunities for the gospel!

Make Me Obedient

Most guys hate being bossed around. I've never enjoyed being told what to do by anybody.

So if you're going to be serious about being a Christian, you're going to have to get over your problem with authority, because as a Christian, God is your authority. This means He is the boss. He calls the shots. We do what He commands because we believe He's smarter than we are.

I've learned something pretty cool over the years. When I ignore that little voice that tells me to do my own thing, and instead choose to obey what God tells me to do, I always benefit from my obedience. But when I disobey, I always pay.

Don't be stubborn. God knows what's best for you, and it's a good idea to do what He says. If you obey Him, He knows He can trust you and He will bless you with even more good things.

God, it's hard to obey You when I have desires
of my own. But I ask You to make me obedient
so I can do all that You've planned for me
to do. Make my desire simple—to listen to
Your voice and obey Your commands.

Make Me an Example

Young guys like you are probably more concerned about finding an older guy you can look to as an example of integrity, hard work, and success than you are about being an example for others of these kinds of good qualities. But I want to challenge you to change your perspective.

What if you began to pray for God to make you an example other young men could follow? What if instead of always hoping and waiting for a godly man to be an example you could look to, you began to live your life in such a way that other guys could start looking at you as a role model they could pattern their life after? It can start today…a brand-new prayer and a brand-new perspective.

Become a leader. Be an example.

God, I present myself to You as weak, sinful,
and imperfect, yet with a desire to be an
example to other guys like me who want
to follow You. Use my life, from today
onward, as an example to be followed.

Make Me like You

From the time I was old enough to remember, I wanted to be like my dad. I wanted to wear work boots like his. I wanted to drive a truck like he did. And I wanted to be a dad like he was to me.

Before long, I was driving a black truck. I had my own pair of boots. And when my son was just four years old, he looked at me and said, "Daddy, when I grow up and have a family, I want to be a daddy just like you because you're the best daddy in the whole world."

There is only one perfect Father. He should be your example of the kind of man you'd like to be one day. Read the Bible and you can start learning what He was like so you can become like Him.

Heavenly Father, make me like You. May I portray Your love, kindness, strength, and mercy to everyone You bring me in contact with. You are my perfect role model.

GOD, GIVE ME...

Give Me Faith

want to help you learn how to ask God for the right things and not feel guilty about it. We can ask Him for things that help us grow as Christians. He wants us to.

Ask God to give you more faith. It's like a muscle, and the more you exercise faith, the stronger it gets. It is the willingness to trust Him and believe He's got your back, no matter what happens. It's hard to have faith when things don't add up or make sense. These are the times when faith becomes reality, because you're asking God for something that you need, but don't have, believing He will do it.

When you pray, have faith God will answer you. When you tithe or give, have faith that He will multiply and use your gift. When you witness, have faith that He will use your story to change a life.

I'm asking You for more faith, Lord. I don't want to settle for a small, boring life. I want to know the adventure of stepping out on a limb in obedience to Your call. Give me faith to believe You.

Give Me Patience

It's a dangerous prayer when you ask God to give you patience. It could mean He allows you to get stuck in rush-hour traffic. Or He could delay that phone call you've been waiting for to find out if you were accepted into the college of your dreams.

But even if it means waiting for five hours at the department of motor vehicles to take your driver's test, you should still ask God to give you patience simply because it's such a necessary trait for life and success. If you want to grow spiritually, it takes time. Like a giant oak tree, your spiritual life doesn't grow big overnight. Patience is one of God's best gifts.

Lord, I don't like to wait. I am by nature impatient and I want things done fast. Will You give me the patience I need to grow deep in my faith and knowledge of You? I know that patience is a virtue, and I ask You to put me in situations where I can learn.

Give Me Your Spirit

The Holy Spirit is not a "thing" or an "it." He is a Person, part of the Trinity, and just as much God as is Jesus or our heavenly Father. So when you repent of your sin and put your trust in Jesus, He sends the Holy Spirit to you to live in you and change you from the inside out. Like when you give your car keys to a friend, we give our lives over to the Spirit and He begins to drive and steer our lives. He has control.

So it makes sense that you would open yourself up to the influence and the transforming power of the Spirit. He is the source of all good things, all the ways you can change into the image of Jesus, and how you can begin to live a victorious life over sin. Ask the Spirit to consume you and fill you every day. Ask Him to speak to you, and tell Him He can have access to any area of your life.

Holy Spirit, I want You to have more control of me; my thoughts, reactions, desires, and dreams. I open myself to Your guidance and I yield myself to Your transforming power. I'm all Yours and I'm all in!

Give Me Opportunity

This is the right age for you to start asking God to give you great opportunities to change the world with His gospel. I started praying that prayer when I was in the eighth grade.

I wanted God to use me! So every morning and every night, I would get down on my knees beside my bed and cry out to God. I would beg him to let me preach, to give me opportunities to witness to my friends, and to open doors for me to travel the world on mission trips.

Guess what? He answered every prayer I prayed. I've preached to over three million people in 45 states and over 30 countries. What kind of opportunities would you like God to give to you? Ask for them!

But in order to take the best opportunities, you will need to say no to the ones that don't serve your mission as a Christian—knowing Jesus and making Him known.

God, I don't want to settle for a boring,
normal life. I want to be Your vessel. Prepare
opportunities for me that I could only dream
of, and when You open the doors, give me
the courage to move forward in faith.

Give Me a Clean Heart

One of the most famous verses in the Bible is Psalm 51:10. King David prays, "Create in me a clean heart, God, and renew a right spirit in me." David understood that only God can cleanse a heart that struggles with sin, darkness, and selfishness.

God cleanses your heart when He saves you, but we also need to allow Him to cleanse our hearts daily, because the temptations we face come at us every day and we fail every day. So we need His cleansing power every day to keep our hearts open and pure. Like when you wash your hands before every meal, Jesus purifies our hearts constantly when we open them up to Him.

Your heart is dirty until you give it to Jesus. Keep giving it to Him every day.

Jesus, I need You to keep working on my heart. Just when I think I'm doing well, I stumble and give in to temptation. I present my heart to You today, and every day, for You to clean up and purify.

Give Me My Identity

As a young man, you're probably tempted to base your identity on things like the sports you play, the girls you date, the friends you hang out with, the car you drive, the gadgets you own, or the grades you make. And while those things may be important, they should never be the basis of your identity as a man.

The only source you can rely on for your identity is your relationship with Christ. Just knowing that God loved you enough to send His Son to die in your place and be raised from death to give you a new life should be the one thing you always think of when you wonder who you are or why you were born. Let God's love give you your identity.

When your identity is based on God's love, you stand on an unshakable foundation.

Father, I don't want to base my identity on the shifting sands of popularity or fading friendships. I want to base it on Your love for me, in spite of my mess-ups and failures. Thank You for always loving me, no matter what.

Give Me Daily Bread

It's kinda hard for guys like us to pray a simple prayer like Jesus told His disciples to pray: "Give us this day our daily bread." That's what poor peasants and farmers prayed in the days of Christ, and it was a simple prayer of survival.

I think this is a good prayer for you, though, because it reminds you to stay humble, remembering that all you need ultimately comes from God. We can't do anything for ourselves, and without God's provision, we'd all starve to death, without even enough bread to make it through a normal day. That's a sobering thought!

God, I admit that I rely on You for everything, even my most basic needs. I ask You for daily bread, enough to sustain me, and to keep me humble at Your feet. I look to You alone as the source of my life and provision for my every need.

PRAYING

Pray Expectantly

We always hear people tell us that we need to pray more, and we know we should. But we struggle with how to get started.

Start by praying expectantly. When you ask God for something, expect Him to keep His promises to you. Expect that He will care for you and give you what you ask according to His will. When you say "amen" you should open your eyes and start looking for His response.

The pastor and missionary George Mueller cared for hundreds of orphans in London. When they ran out of food, they would set the table with plates and utensils, then bow their heads and pray for God to supply food. Over and over again, He met their needs in miraculous and unexplainable ways.

God has the unlimited resources of the universe at His disposal. Expect Him to answer and provide for you.

*Father, grant me an imagination by which I
envision You actually answering my prayers
for Your glory in ways that amaze everyone.
Give me an attitude of expectancy.*

Pray Regularly

Did you know that it takes about seven weeks to break a bad habit?

It takes that long for the neural pathways in your brain to reformat themselves. So if you stop biting your nails for seven weeks, in theory you've broken the habit. Interestingly enough, it takes the same amount of time to form a new habit.

Prayer is a must, but it takes time to get into the habit of praying. I try to pray all day long—before meals, before meetings, in the car, with my kids, and when I wake up and am still in bed.

Try praying regularly. Set a goal to pray three or four times a day, then increase it to ten times a day. Before you know it, you're praying all the time and it becomes a habit, almost like breathing.

Jesus, teach me how to make prayer like a second language by practicing it regularly throughout my day. And when I find myself worrying or stressing out over a test or a paper or a relationship, I want that to trigger a response in my mind to choose to pray at that moment.

Pray Specifically

Lots of your prayers are probably a little stale and generic. I know mine can become boring and predictable.

"God bless my family. Be with everyone today. Thank you for food and clothes and my house." That's a good place to start, but try being more specific when you pray. Call out people by name to God. Ask for things in detail.

Once I needed $2000 to pay for a mission trip to India, and I was leaving in five days. I prayed specifically, and two individuals sent me personal checks for $1000 each, paying the exact amount I needed.

It won't always turn out that exact, but it's important that you bring every single need and all the details to God. He loves coming through for you, because He gets the glory and you get a cool story to tell!

*I have lots of specific needs in my life, Lord.
From today forward, I will not be embarrassed
to ask You specifically for those things, and
when You come through, I will tell everyone
what You've done so You may be glorified.*

Pray Personally

On a flight one time, I sat beside a Christian from a different tradition, and we began talking about prayer. I told him I tried to pray as a habit, all day long. He couldn't believe I would just pray anywhere, about anything, all the time. He actually liked the idea of thinking about prayer like a personal conversation between friends.

Don't use big, religious words when you pray. Make it personal and real. Just start by telling God what's on your mind, the things you're worried about, and how you're feeling. Making it personal helps you open up, and it builds trust.

My little boy prayed one time, "God, help my daddy because he's in a really bad mood, and I am too." That's how you make it personal!

Sometimes I get so formal when I pray, but I know I don't have to make it some big ritual. Jesus, I want us to be close, personal friends, and I want my prayers to sound like I am talking to my best friend, because I am.

Pray Radically

It's easy to pray safe prayers that don't really challenge your faith. It's okay to pray for God to be with all the poor people and heal all the sick people, but there's more to prayer than you might think.

You're actually talking to the God who made the universe. Pray bigger, crazier prayers, not for the sake of being weird, but for the sake of His glory! Ask Him to do miraculous, unexplainable, life-changing things. Pray for lost people to be saved. Ask Him to anoint you to preach the gospel to people who've never heard it. Pray for Muslim, Hindu, and Buddhist nations to open their doors to the church and missionaries. Ask big, because God can do big things. It's not really that radical when you think about it after all.

I don't want to spend the rest of my life praying generic, boring prayers. I want to have a greater faith for greater things, because I know that You are a great God who can radically blow my mind! Show up and show off, Lord.

Pray Constantly

Don't think of prayer as a formal religious ritual. Think of prayer as a constant conversation.

It will help you pray more effectively if you look at prayer as an ongoing, never-ending talk with a good friend. You probably have a really close friend that you call or text or e-mail all the time. You never really stop communicating with them. It's ongoing.

That's a good way to look at prayer. You should be talking to God all day long, about everything that's happening, both good and bad—thanking Him, sharing with Him how you feel, and praying for others. Don't think that your prayer is over because you say "amen." Pray constantly, and keep the lines of communication open.

> *I want to talk to You all day about all that's going on around me, Lord. I know that if I pray constantly, it will help me feel closer to You and more connected to You as my friend.*

Pray Honestly

This may shock you—but I really think that your prayers should be brutally, gut-wrenchingly honest.

Jesus was honest with His Father when He prayed the night before He was crucified. David was honest when he prayed in his psalms. God already knows what you're hiding from Him anyway, so what's the use in holding back? Tell Him the truth. Lay your soul bare before Him. Once you do this a few times, you will realize He won't destroy you with lightning bolts for being real, and you will feel more comfortable with an honest approach to prayer.

Try it the next time you pray. Not only will it refresh your heart, you will also feel better emotionally knowing there are no secrets between you and God.

Lord, teach me to tell You the truth when I talk
to You. Help me remember that You see and
know everything anyway. I need to trust You
more, and honesty in prayer is a great way to start.

Pray Openly

We enjoy a lot of freedoms here in America that other people around the world will never experience. One of them is the freedom of religion. You can express your faith in Jesus openly, in public, without worrying about being arrested or locked up for it.

I've been able to share Jesus with people just because I prayed before a meal in a restaurant. I've had parents tell me they appreciate my praying with my family before we leave on a plane flight. Sometimes praying openly is a witness to others.

I encourage you to take every opportunity to publicly, openly bow your head in prayer—not to draw attention to yourself, but to show others that a young man isn't ashamed to pray to God even when there are other people around.

I'm not ashamed to be seen publicly praying to You, Jesus. Give me the courage to show others by my example that they can also pray openly.

Pray Responsively

You will get so much more out of your time reading Scripture if you will follow up reading the Bible with praying about what you've just read.

In other words, respond to what you read with prayer. Be responsive to God's Word by talking back to Him. If you read a verse that convicts you, respond by praying a prayer of repentance. If you're reminded of how good God has been to you, respond in prayer with praise and rejoicing. If you're feeling discouraged, respond by asking God to give you hope and comfort.

You respond in class when your teacher asks you a question. You respond to your mom and dad when they tell you to do something. You respond to your coaches when they give you an assignment. Did you know that God is always talking to you? And every time you respond to Him, it's a prayer.

God, help me do more than just read the Bible and sing songs. I want to be intimately involved in Your mission to redeem this world, so I want to be more responsive to Your voice and Your guidance.

Pray Defensively

When you get into an argument with a friend, a coach, your parents, or just about anyone, you usually want to prove that you're right and they're wrong. And when anyone challenges you, the natural response is to defend yourself with your words.

The bad news is, you can't defend yourself against things more powerful than you—temptation, satanic attack, lust, fear. Your only hope is prayer, and prayer is your only defense, because it's how you approach God when you need Him to get your back.

Pray defensively. When you feel helpless or out of control, go straight to God and ask Him to come to your defense. Don't try to fight your enemies by yourself. They will win. Let God defend you. Call on His name in your time of trouble.

God, I consciously acknowledge that You're the only true defense I will ever have against the lies and accusations of Satan. I will run to You when I'm afraid, angry, or hurt. Praying to You is my best defense when I'm being attacked.

GIVING

Give Sacrificially

God is a giver. He gave us life. He gave us His Son. He gives us forgiveness.

If you want to be a man of God, it starts by learning how to give like God gives.

He gave sacrificially when He sent Jesus to take our place on the cross. What can you give to Him that would be that powerful? Nothing! But He doesn't want you to try and match His sacrifice. He only wants you to give in response to His giving. So start by offering Him what you have—your life.

Your life is a living sacrifice to God. In the Old Testament, an animal wasn't a sacrifice until it was dead. You're dead to your sin when you repent and trust Jesus, but you're also made alive by His grace. Your life is a gift, and you give it back to God as a sacrifice.

Lord Jesus, I lay my life down to You. I also offer You my time, my money, and my affections. I want to give sacrificially as a man who's already dead to sin and alive in Christ.

Give Immediately

My ninth-grade Bible teacher used to always tell us, "Delayed obedience is disobedience."

When you see a need and you can meet it, don't delay. Do it fast. Give immediately.

If you can learn how to give when you're young (before you have a lot of money and possessions), you will keep giving as you get older, and it will be a lesson you carry with you for the rest of your life. But you also need to learn how to give immediately, without any hesitation.

Practically, make sure you keep some cash in your wallet, because you never know when you'll meet someone who needs help. Always take an offering with you when you go to church so you get in the habit of giving. Give your coat away to a guy with no coat.

Look for ways to give immediately and you will find them because they're everywhere.

I don't want to even hesitate when You show me a need, Jesus. I want to give immediately because I know if I hesitate, my selfishness is likely to kick in and tempt me to not give at all.

Give Cheerfully

The apostle Paul, the greatest evangelist and church planter who ever lived, had a lot to say about giving. For him, it was all about the attitude.

He's sort of famous for the phrase, "God loves a cheerful giver." That simply means your attitude when you give should be happy, joyful, excited, and glad.

Why would you get excited about giving your money or your stuff away? Because your generosity is God's way of providing for the needs of other people. How awesome to think that He is using your generosity to build His kingdom on this earth! That should inspire you not only to give more, but to give with an attitude of ridiculous joy and uncontrollable excitement.

*Help me be mindful of my attitude when someone
asks me to give, whether my money or my time,
because I know that the attitude of my heart
when I give is just as important as the gift I give.*

Give Consistently

One thing I respected about my dad was how he always gave when he saw a need. When he was living in a nursing home during the final days of his life, he asked me to send money from his account to a missionary in Central America. It would help the man buy a jeep that would allow him to reach churches in a remote area where only a four-wheel-drive could get to. He was still giving, even on his deathbed.

My dad gave consistently, throughout his life. He began when he was young and he started with a tithe. *Tithe* simply means "a tenth." So when you get an allowance or a paycheck, the first 10 percent goes to your local church. Beyond that, you get to decide how much more you want to give God.

You become consistent in giving by practicing it. The more you give, the easier it becomes and the better you get at it.

Jesus, I don't want to be sporadic in how I give. I want to be consistent, in the same way You were faithful to Your mission. Teach me to begin with the tithe as a discipline of giving.

Give Disproportionately

Disproportionately is a big word, but you probably know what it means. If you made a good grade on a research project and your instructor gave you $1 million, the reward would be disproportionate to the achievement.

But if you think about it, that's what God did for us by giving us life and forgiveness when we deserved judgment and wrath. Just as He gave us more than He should have, now when you give, you're following His example. It's not a requirement. It's an invitation!

Try giving more than you think you can afford. Give more than just the tithe. Go above and beyond. Support missionaries and church planters. Support a child through World Vision or Compassion International. Be like Jesus by giving more than is required.

Just like You gave it all for me, Jesus, I give
You control over all areas of my life, including
my money. It may be difficult, but I want to
give more than I have to, because You showed
me the example when You died for me.

Give Secretly

Jesus once told His followers, "Don't do your good deeds publicly, to be admired by others...when you give to someone in need, don't let your left hand know what your right hand is doing" (Matthew 6:1 NLT). There were people in His day who loved to show off when they gave to God. Jesus was not impressed with them because their hearts were in the wrong place. They were giving publicly so others would think they were godly.

Jesus wants to remind you that you shouldn't take pride in the amount you give, or the proportion you give. It's between you and God, and it's not for show. Your motivation for giving matters as much as the actual gift you give.

Don't become proud of the amount you give. Don't announce it to others. Do it secretly, trusting that God sees and knows the size of your gift, but more importantly, that He sees the attitude of your heart when you give it.

God, purify my motives for giving. Help me remember I am giving to You, and You know the reasons I give as surely as You know the amount.

Give Carefully

As you learn how to make giving a part of your life, make sure that you use wisdom as you decide where to give beyond your local church.

It's sad to say, but the truth is, there are organizations and ministries that ask you for your money, but they may not be completely honest about where your money goes. That's why it's so important for you to give carefully. Do your homework, ask questions, do an online search, talk to your pastor, and find out what the most respectable and trusted ministries are. Then you can make a good decision about where you sow and invest, and you can feel good knowing your money won't be wasted but will go toward helping the poor, providing clean water, rescuing kids from human trafficking, or proclaiming the gospel to those who've never heard.

God, I don't want to be critical, I want to be careful. Give me discernment as I choose the right ministries to invest in.

Give Offensively

I know…I need to explain this, right? Give "offensively"? How do you do that?

You're going to be tempted to get greedy as you get older. Our culture revolves around making more and gaining more, not giving more away. So it would seem like common sense as a Christian to try and "defend" yourself against the love of money and greed. But I think there's a better way to avoid getting sucked into the greed vacuum.

Don't play defense. Play offense. Don't wait on greed to attack you and then try to defend yourself. Go on the offensive! Do it by giving offensively. Generosity is the cure for the disease of greed, so every time you give, you are fighting back the tendency and temptation to be greedy. Every time you give, you are playing offense, not defense.

Father, give me a new perspective on what happens inside my heart when I give, and remind me that every time I practice generosity, I'm defeating greed and selfishness.

Give Patiently

One of my favorite chapters in the Bible is Galatians 6. It reminds us not to give up when we get tired of doing good and right things, because eventually we will see great results of our obedience and faithfulness.

It's easy to get discouraged when you're giving your time and your energy to something God wants you to do, but you haven't seen any fruit yet. You'll be tempted to give up. But don't give in and don't give up. Keep giving, keep serving, keep reading your Bible, and keep praying.

Be patient as you sow and give and invest. Just like it takes time for a kernel to become a stalk full of corn, it takes time to see how your giving will turn into fruit for the gospel. Just wait patiently, and keep giving while you wait. When the time is right, you will see what God can do with what you give Him.

Teach me patience, Lord, while I wait on the results of my obedient giving. I trust that the results are all up to You, so I will wait patiently until You're ready to show me what You want me to see.

Give Totally

We've been talking a lot about how to give to God, but there is one word that sums it all up.

Totally. God doesn't want your money. He wants your heart. And if He has your heart, He has all of you, totally.

Everything you have belongs to God. It came from Him, He could take it from you if He wanted to, or He could give you even more. When you realize that 100 percent of your money, your possessions, and your abilities belong to God, it's easier to give Him what He asks for. You're just a manager. He's the owner.

Giving is not how God gets the money out of your pockets. Giving is how God gets the idols out of your heart. It reminds us that our faith is in Jesus Christ, not bank accounts or paychecks. Giving continuously forces you to face selfishness and greed and choose Jesus and generosity instead. So give totally. Hold nothing back from the Lord.

Here and now, Lord Jesus, I declare that all I am and all I have are completely Yours, and I offer it totally to You. I'm all Yours, and I'm all in!

TRUTH, NOT FEELINGS

Only So Much

It's so easy to get busy and even easier to stay busy once you get there. The more tasks and jobs and opportunities you take on, the more worried and stressed and tired you'll get. There will always be stuff to do, and you'll never be totally caught up. You have to say no sometimes, even to good things.

There's only so much you can do. You're not Superman and you're not a super-Christian. You have limits. You need rest and you need to prioritize the things that matter most. Guys like to feel important by accomplishing a lot, but it can lead to burnout and fatigue. Be careful that you're not doing more than you're capable of, because eventually it will catch up with you.

God doesn't want you to do everything. Even He rested after He created the world.

Lord, I know that You don't expect me to do more than I'm capable of doing. When I get overwhelmed, I will remember that You loved me before I was even born, and I will rest in that love.

Owning Up

It's a lot easier to blame somebody else than to take responsibility when you've dropped the ball. Our country is full of this mentality, from politicians to movie stars to criminals.

Real men of God own up to their mistakes. They don't point fingers at others. They don't make excuses. They stand up straight and admit where they've failed, they ask for another chance, and they learn from their mistakes so they do better next time.

Our example is Jesus Christ. He didn't suffer for His mistakes—He suffered for ours. He didn't make excuses for Himself—He made a way for us to be saved. Remember that all your sins and mistakes have already been taken care of, so own up when you mess up, and learn to be a man of God in doing so.

God, it's time for me to grow up by owning up. By Your grace, I will not blame others when the mistake was mine. I will learn from my failures and the consequences of them so I can become a true man of God.

Making Things Right

It's one thing to own up to your mess-ups. It's a whole other level to make the first move by making things right if your mistake has hurt or affected someone else.

Swallow hard, take a deep breath, and decide that you will initiate the process of making things right if you've offended or hurt a brother or sister in Christ. It may mean a phone call, a hard face-to-face conversation, or even the involvement of a pastor or a leader. If it costs you time or money or both, do it anyway. Simply because it's the right thing.

God wants His children to live in love and unity. Even if you feel it's not your fault, be the bigger man and try to make things right.

God, it's so hard to make the first move in making things right, but that's exactly what You did for me, dying in my place before I ever even repented of my sin. I will follow Your example.

Swallowing Pride

I grew up in the country, on a farm, and all my friends liked to fight. Actually, the worst fights I ever got into were with my best friends. We always got over it quickly and let it go. But when I became a teenager and gave my life to Jesus, I noticed that I didn't feel right about fighting anymore. I knew it was not what Jesus wanted me to do.

Then I got into a huge fistfight with a guy at school over something stupid. My coach broke us up. He didn't say anything to the other guys, but he pulled me into his office and said, "Clayton, you're a Christian now and you say God's called you to preach. This is a chance for you to swallow your pride and apologize, even if it wasn't your fault."

I will never forget how hard it was to make the decision to apologize but how free I felt when I did it. Don't be stubborn. You're not perfect. Swallow your pride every chance you get.

> *Jesus, when I reflect on how much You saved me from, it's a lot easier to be humble. Don't let me ever forget that.*

The Power of an Apology

Why is it so hard to just say "I'm sorry"?

It's hard because we're sinners who never want to admit we're wrong. The truth is, though, we're all wrong, all the time. And usually when you're having trouble with your parents, co-workers, teammates, or friends, the first step toward patching things up are the two simple words "I'm sorry."

This communicates to the other person that you care about the relationship. You want things to be okay. And even if you're not totally in the wrong, you can still say that you're sorry that the relationship has suffered and you want to get things straightened out.

This also works with Jesus. The first step toward repentance is to feel sorrow for your sin, knowing it breaks God's heart and hurts your relationship. Just say you're sorry. Get it over with. It's not that hard with some practice.

Every day, God, I have much to be sorry for, but when I repent, I also have much to be thankful for. Thank You for accepting my apology and receiving my repentance.

Not Really Feeling It

Let's talk about your feelings."

Ha-ha! That sounds like something you'd hear a gang of girls say at a sleepover. But guys have feelings and emotions, and it's dangerous when we don't want to admit how much our feelings control what we say and do.

Your feelings cannot be trusted, because they change all the time. You may be mad enough to hit someone, but if you hit them, you go to jail, so you choose not to hit them. And sometimes, when you know you need to pray, get in the Word, or keep a promise, you might not feel like doing it right then. I've heard so many guys say, "I'm not really feeling it."

A man of God chooses to do the right thing even when he's not feeling it. Don't wait until you feel like following Jesus to follow Jesus. Be His obedient disciple regardless of how you feel, and pretty soon you will be feeling it.

Jesus, I need help when I don't feel like resisting temptation or when I don't want to do things Your way. I want to live by faith, not feelings.

Fickle Feelings

It's a really bad idea to make decisions when you're feeling a strong emotion, like anger or jealousy or excitement. You can do something in the heat of the moment that you will regret for the rest of your life. I met a guy who served 15 years in prison because he punched a guy who insulted him, and the guy fell over, hit his head, and died. He wasn't trying to kill the other guy. He just let his feelings control him instead of controlling his feelings.

Your feelings are fickle. Don't trust them. They're like fog and smoke—they come and go and appear and disappear quickly. Instead, learn to trust the Holy Spirit. He lives in you. He guides you. He restrains you when you're angry, encourages you when you're sad, and tries to stop you before you fly off the handle and make a big mess out of some small thing. Replace your fickle feelings with the presence of the Spirit of God.

Holy Spirit, I acknowledge Your presence in my life and Your residence in my heart. Speak loudly and clearly. Yell at me if You have to.

Forsaking Feelings

Since you know your feelings are fickle, I encourage you to deal with them appropriately when they're telling you to do something wrong or sinful.

Forsake your fickle feelings. Choose something that's stable and solid instead. Get out your Bible and read what God says. He's not unpredictable and unstable like your emotions. His Word has stood for thousands of years and has led millions of people away from the edge of destruction. Let go of the desire to get mad, get ahead, or get even, and go get your Bible. God will meet you on those pages and in those words on those pages. It's happened to me thousands of times since I became a Christian.

It will happen to you too.

God, when I'm in the heat of the moment, please come to me at that moment and lead me back to Your truth and Your Word. I know I can't trust my emotions, but I know I can trust You completely.

MAKING REPLACEMENTS

Replacing Fear with Faith

Faith replaces fear, but not without a fight. Even the toughest, strongest men live with fear— fear of failure, fear of being alone, fear of embarrassment, fear of not being good enough.

Fear will control your life unless you replace it with something better and stronger. Faith can live where fear now resides. But you can't reason with fear or talk it into leaving. You have to evict it. And it won't go without a fight.

Each time you feel fear overtake you, you can replace it with faith. Pray a short prayer like this out loud…

Jesus, I am afraid right now and I'm about to freak out. I need You to give me faith. I choose to trust in You right now, even though all I can feel is fear. I believe that You can replace fear with faith, and I choose to believe You right now. I listen to Your voice, and I ignore the voices that make me feel afraid.

Replacing Envy with Excellence

Envy is another word for jealousy, and most guys get jealous when they see another guy with something they wish they had. It could be a girlfriend, a car, nicer gadgets, a job, a college scholarship, a better family, popularity, opportunity, bigger muscles…you know what I'm talking about here.

How do you replace envy? With excellence!

Stop living a lazy, mediocre life and pursue excellence in everything. Get up early. Stop eating junk food. Exercise more. Read and study instead of playing video games for three hours. Quit envying what others have and make your life count for something.

Excellence doesn't happen overnight. It happens over time. And the sooner you start, the faster you will replace jealousy with excellence in your own life.

God, help me recognize how envious I get when others succeed. And instead of staying jealous of them, grant me the strength to begin striving for excellence as a man of God.

Replacing Performance with Purpose

Our culture is obsessed with entertainment, so the people who perform for our entertainment become larger than life. We make them famous and rich. Then normal people like you and me are tempted to move into "performance mode" because we know performers get noticed.

There's something better than performance, and it's purpose. When you believe that God made you for a reason, that you're not an accident of nature, and that your life matters, you will take each day more seriously and make each decision more wisely.

Purpose is better than performance, because performers pretend for crowds of strangers. You, however, live out your purpose for an audience of One—the God who knows you better than you know yourself.

God, show me Your purpose for my life, and
by faith, I will live each day for Your glory
and fame, not my own. I know I don't
have to perform to earn Your love.

Replacing Insecurity with Identity

Okay, here's an awkward confession. I started losing my hair when I was 19. It's weird to be a sophomore in college and always be checking the mirror to see how many more follicles have said goodbye.

For the first time in my life, I became insecure about how I looked. And I became embarrassed at how insecure I became about my thinning hairline. So I had to come face-to-face with who I really was—did I base my feelings on my outer appearance or my inner identity?

You can replace your insecurities with a solid, unshakable identity as a child of God who doesn't have to prove anything or measure up to anyone's expectations. Jesus measured up where you fell short. Now, you're all good. Identify yourself with Jesus, not appearance or performance.

Jesus, I find security in Your perfect, complete love for me. No matter how I look or what others think, I belong to You. You are my identity.

Replacing Guilt with Grace

God has wired you to know the difference between right and wrong, and when you choose wrong, it feels wrong inside. It's called conviction, but if you don't repent when you feel that conviction, it turns into guilt. Like when you allow a cut to become infected because you didn't clean it, guilt infects your mind, and you begin to doubt God's love and your own salvation.

Replace guilt with grace. Grace is better because it assures you that God has pardoned your sin, forgiven you, and been kind to you even when you didn't deserve it. Guilt says, "Do more," but grace says, "It's already done."

Guilt says, "Try harder and God will love you." Grace says, "Surrender more because God loves you."

I hate living with guilt, Jesus. I want to live by Your grace, which I didn't have to earn and don't have to work for. I take it as a free gift. Thank You for grace!

Replacing Status with Service

got bumped to first class once on a flight, and I sat beside a man who was really rude to the flight attendant. He kept bossing her around and being ugly toward her. He was acting like a jerk! When I asked him why he was so mean to her, he told me that he had achieved "platinum status" with the airlines because he flew so much, and that her job was to serve him. She was getting paid by him, so she should serve him.

Don't be like that guy. Status is a joke, and you can lose it as fast as you get it. Power and popularity fade fast. But a Christian is first of all a servant, just like Jesus. He served us. We should serve Him and others.

Don't chase status. Replace it with service. When you serve someone, you look like Jesus.

Jesus, I want to look for every chance I can find to serve others in Your name. Whether sweeping floors, taking out trash, scrubbing toilets, or helping with chores, I choose service over status.

Replacing Sarcasm with Celebration

Most of the humor in our culture, on TV, and in the movies is not actually funny. It's just crude and sarcastic. Sarcasm is getting a laugh at the expense of another person, and while you may look funny for a minute, you will drive away real relationships with people because no one wants to be close to a sarcastic person. You never know when they'll say something mean, so you don't trust them.

Choose celebration over sarcasm. Instead of using your words to belittle others, use them to build them up, encourage them, and celebrate the good things that happen to them.

I try to use Facebook and Twitter to publicly celebrate the victories of others. And I know that my best friends, the ones I trust the most, are the ones who will celebrate good things with me.

Be that kind of guy. Kill sarcasm and choose celebration.

Holy Spirit, rein in my tongue and give me strength to use my words for celebrating Your goodness to others, just like I'd want those others to celebrate Your goodness to me.

Replacing Criticism with Creativity

Sir Winston Churchill, the famous prime minister of Great Britain, once said, "It is much easier to criticize, because it is much more difficult to create." He'd faced his fair share of criticism before leading his country through the horrors of World War II. He understood that lazy people like to criticize the hard work and good deeds of those who are actually willing to do something.

Don't be a critic. Be a creator. Make something that God can use. Write a great book, direct a great movie, invent the next big thing, start the next Microsoft or Apple Computers. If you have time to criticize others, then you have time to create something yourself.

Use the mind God gave you to make the world a better place. And if you can't say something good, don't say anything.

God, I confess that when I criticize others, it's
a sign of my own insecurity and jealousy.
Change me from the inside out so I can make
this world better and bring You glory.

Replacing Worry with Worship

When you worry, you are actually indirectly telling God you don't think He can handle a situation you're going through. You're telling Him that your problem is too big for Him.

The opposite of worry is worship. Worship is the simple act of giving your mind's attention and your heart's affection to Jesus. When you quit looking at the source of your worry and look at Jesus, your worship reminds you of all He has already done. Then you realize how useless it is to worry about anything. You have a history, a long record that you can look at to prove that God will come through.

Replace worry, immediately, with worship. Speak out loud and remember His grace to you. Worship will eat worry for lunch.

Lord, I choose to worship You in the middle of
all my worries and anxiety. Give me more faith
by reminding me of Your miracles in my life.

Replacing Fantasy with Reality

Take a look around and you'll see people living in a fantasy world, where you can spend more money than you make, get a free ride from the government, eat all you want, and party like there's no tomorrow. Beer commercials and TV infomercials support this fantasy world.

You need to replace fantasy with reality. In the real world, there are consequences to actions. There are bills that must be paid, jobs you have to go to, and heart disease, diabetes, and other sicknesses that result from eating junk. And girls have babies when they have sex with boys.

God desperately wants young men like you to lead the way in a culture that doesn't want to live in reality. Look at the outcome of a decision before you make it and choose wisely before you act.

I know I live in a broken world, Father, and I want to be a part of Your restoration of all things. Help me see things as they really are.

Replacing Apathy with Ambition

There was a guy on my high-school football team we all used to joke about. He never once got his uniform dirty, because he never actually played in a game, because he never participated in practice, because he was lazy. That is called apathy.

Apathy will eventually kill everything good in a man. We need a reason to get up in the morning. God has given us a redeemed ambition, not to live life for wealth and pleasure, but to give our lives to Him to be used as He sees fit.

Make it your ambition to be a mighty man of God, humbly surrendered to His purposes. Don't be lazy. Replace apathy with godly ambition.

God, make me ambitious for Your gospel, for Your kingdom, for Your purpose, for Your presence, and for the lost to be found by Your love and salvation.

CHOOSING

Power to Choose

You make hundreds of choices every day, from what you wear to where you eat lunch to the music you listen to in your car. These seem like small things.

You also have the power to choose to honor God in every single big decision you make. Choose what to do based on the answer to a simple question: *What choice would bring God more glory and make me more like Jesus?*

Should you go to college now? Where? Who should you marry? What should you major in? What job should you take? There may be various outcomes to your decisions, but if you decide based on what will help you grow and bring God glory, you will choose the right thing.

Lord, I don't always trust myself to make the
right choice, so I will trust in Your Spirit
to guide me through every hard decision
I face. I only want what You want.

Choose to Grow

Most guys stop growing physically between the ages of 17 and 20. I was six-foot-one in the eighth grade. I'm glad I stopped growing at about 225 pounds.

However, you never want to stop growing spiritually. God wants you to keep learning and changing on the inside. The Bible calls this "transformation," and it's the way God keeps challenging you and shaping you into the image of Jesus.

Change is a choice. Choose to keep growing and changing. If you stay connected to Jesus, He's like a vine that gives life and nutrients to the branches that bear fruit (read about it in John 15). You grow slowly with every small word and action and decision you make. Keep growing!

Jesus, I want to stay connected to You so You can keep changing me as a man. I want to grow into a man of God and I want to look like You!

Choose Rest

The lyrics to an old song by the Eagles tell how they used to hurry and "worry a lot"…but it just didn't work and it was "high time I quit it." I guess they learned a lesson that all guys need to learn.

Rest is not a sign of weakness. It's a sign of being human. We get wrapped up in life and work and play and projects, and we abuse the minds and bodies God gave us. If we abuse them for too long, we will lose them. And you only get one body in this life. If you ruin it, you don't get another one until Jesus comes back.

The Bible says those who won't work are lazy, but those who won't rest are disobedient. Even Jesus rested, many times going off alone to get away from the craziness. If He needed it, don't you think you do too?

Jesus, I choose to rest, believing that You are in control of the world without my help. I want to be on this earth for a long time doing the things You want me to accomplish, and rest will help get me there.

Choose Purity

The good news...God gave you a desire for a wife, and the desire to be intimate with her physically. Yes, I'm talking about sex. You knew that.

The hard news...He doesn't want you to give in to those desires until you're mature and ready to be a husband, even though you've wanted to have sex since you were in sixth or seventh grade.

The really good news...with God's help, you can choose purity over passion. You don't have to cave in to sexual desires like some kind of animal. You can create boundaries, draw lines, find accountability, and rely on God to keep you pure until you've met a godly woman you can spend your life with.

By God's grace, my wife and I were virgins when we got married. Even if you're not, you can still choose purity. It's never too late.

I have such strong desires as a man, and there's no way I can control them without Your help, God. I will choose to yield myself to Your plan for my purity.

Choose Encouragement

I absolutely love being friends with guys who encourage me. My lifelong best friend, Brian, never calls me unless he says something that lifts me up and lets me know he believes in me. I love hanging out with him.

Why not be an encourager like that? Choose to be the guy who gives hope and courage to his brothers. You will always be rich with friends if you learn how to be an encouragement.

But what if *you* need encouraging? What if you struggle sometimes with sadness and discouragement? The easiest way to find encouragement for yourself is to give it to others. It takes your attention off yourself and places it on others—then you realize you don't have it so bad after all.

Choose encouragement. Everyone will be glad you did, including you.

Lord, make me an encourager. Show me a way to lift up my brothers and sisters in Christ.

Choose Loyalty

Early in my ministry, someone wrongly accused me of saying a curse word from the stage during a sermon. I had a friend named Steven who brought this accusation to me, and when I told him it wasn't true, he went to the source and not only set him straight, but made sure he set the record straight with everyone he'd lied to.

That's called loyalty. Did you know Steven is still one of my best friends today, more than a decade later? Do you even have to wonder why I still love and trust him? It's simple—he's a loyal friend.

Choose to be loyal to those you love, beginning with Jesus. Be ready and willing to sacrifice and serve those you're loyal to. Don't abandon people when things get hard. Stick with them. Stay by their side. Let them know that you've got their back, no matter what.

God, make me a loyal friend, a real disciple,
and a trustworthy ambassador of Your
love to the world. Help me stay loyal even
when it would be easier to bail out.

Choose Self-Respect

Don't misunderstand me...apart from Jesus, there's really nothing that awesome about you or me.

But God loves you and made you in His image, so you need to live and act like you belong to the King of kings. Choose self-respect.

Some practical ways to do this include dressing appropriately, speaking clearly, using good grammar, showing up early to appointments, being prepared for school projects, working to make good grades, sitting on the front row in class and at church, picking good friends, avoiding bad influences, spending money wisely, honoring your parents, cleaning up after yourself, not wasting food, taking care of your car, paying your bills on time, working a full day without taking advantage of your boss, telling the truth about yourself on social media, and keeping your commitments.

These things make you a better man.

I don't want to be a typical lazy guy who refuses to grow up. I want to be Your man, a man You can trust with big things. Give me a healthy dose of self-respect as I mature in Christ.

Choose Honor

This is a concept you've probably never been taught about. We don't like to honor people because we think it's arrogant of anyone to expect honor. They have to earn it first!

Respect is earned, but honor is given. We honor those who lead us based on their position, not on their performance. I may not agree with all the policies of the president of the United States, but I honor him and his office, and if he walked into the room, I would stand up to give him honor. So would you.

We honor our leaders by praying for them, by refusing to spread gossip and rumors about them, and by choosing to give them the benefit of the doubt instead of assuming the worst.

You will never become a true leader if you don't choose to honor leaders.

God, I choose to honor those You've placed in leadership over me. In doing so, I choose to believe the best about them, understanding how tough it is to be in their place of leadership.

Choose the Bible

Your world is filled with 6 squillion distractions. Texts, e-mail, Twitter, YouTube, Facebook, iTunes, TV, Instagram, Vimeo, ESPN, projects, and friends. You can take your pick as to what gets your attention. You can choose from among countless options.

You should choose the Bible. It's more important than every other option. It's not a trend or a fad. It won't be replaced by the next big thing, ever. And it's the only thing you can know for sure that will speak to your heart, directly on behalf of God.

The Bible comforts you when you're hurting, and it hurts you when you're too comfortable. It's not fazed by elections or revolts, wars or natural disasters, and it doesn't care who's hot and who's not. Choose the Bible, every day.

Lord, I know that I can't know You if I don't know Your Word, and I can't know Your Word if I don't choose to read it and submit to it every day. Help me make Your Word my first priority.

Choose Your Influencers

When you have an impact on someone, you are an influence on them. When they have an impact on you, they are an influencer in your life.

You need to choose your influencers carefully. Do you form your worldview from the right sources? What powers and people influence you? Compare the amount of time you spend playing video games to time you spend in God's Word. Compare the amount of time you spend watching TV to the time you spend in prayer. Or compare the amount of money you give to your church to the amount of money you spend on entertainment and fast food.

Are you being influenced by the right voices? Who are you listening to? Turn off the bad influencers and tune into the ones that show you who God is and what He is like.

Lord, help me get serious about the powers that influence my life, even if it means cutting off some relationships or getting rid of some things I've grown attached to.

BIG SECRETS

Big Secret: Get Up Early

Sometimes people ask me if I have some big secret to being successful as a writer and a pastor. I actually have more than one. I'd like to share some of the biggest with you. If you've made it this far in the book, I'm assuming you're seriously pursuing a godly life, and I believe you'll apply these truths.

If you want to accomplish more than the average guy, you need to get up early. It's the most practical thing that all leaders do. It shows discipline. It gives you a jump on the day. While others are sleeping, you're getting ahead. You won't feel rushed so you'll make fewer mistakes. It's also the quietest part of the day, when your mind is alert and you can have good time alone with God. I learned this from my dad—maybe you can learn it from me.

> *Jesus, I know this will be hard, but will You please help me begin getting up early so I can give You the first part of my day before I get busy with everything else that's going on?*

Big Secret: Go to Bed

In high school and college I got into the really bad habit of staying up late. It took me years to replace this with going to bed early, but it has made a huge difference in my life.

Honestly, nothing good or healthy or productive happens late at night. God made your body to get tired a little after dark. That's when you should go to bed, or shortly thereafter. If you stay up late, what are you doing? Playing video games. Surfing the Web. Wasting time doing stupid stuff. Or you're sinning...looking at porn, flirting with a bad girl on Facebook, or watching something useless on cable or satellite.

Stop drinking energy drinks, turn off all electronics at 9 or 10 p.m., and go to bed. You'll get up earlier, get ahead of everyone else, find your body's natural rhythm, and be ready for God to use you. Or you could keep playing video games...and never grow up.

God, simply put, I want to grow up, and it starts by saying no to the dumb things that distract me and waste time. Help me care for my body and mind by going to bed.

Big Secret: Sit Up Front

Here's a big secret that I swear by. No matter where you are, always sit on the front row. Head straight to the front and sit right in the middle. It shows that you're hungry and serious about learning and listening.

You may think that's silly, but I assure you it's not. It worked for me. My dad made me start doing this in second grade when I got a bad grade. I kept doing it all through middle school and high school, and by the time I got to college, it was so ingrained in me I didn't have to think about it, I just went straight to the front.

I graduated high school with a perfect GPA. I received a college scholarship worth about $50,000 and I graduated college with a perfect GPA. I also received the "Outstanding Graduate of the Year" award. So do I think sitting on the front row is the reason I did so well?

Yes, I do. It made me take education seriously, and it impressed my teachers and professors. Now, try it!

Okay, Lord—it seems odd, but I commit to You that when I can, I will sit up front with an open mind, as a way to discipline me to pay attention.

Big Secret: Look Them in the Eyes

My dad was a farmer and a small businessman. He dealt with people face-to-face all day, every day, for nearly 50 years. And he always made eye contact with people. He looked them square in the eyes.

When you do that, you let people know they can trust you, but you also learn how to read people. You can tell so much about someone by watching them, their facial expressions, and where their eyes go. Most communication is nonverbal. Learn to watch people. Look them in the eye when you talk to them.

I encourage you to spend less time online and on your phone and to spend more time interacting with real people, the kind with skin on. Jesus took on flesh so He could live among people. People matter more than anything. Become familiar with them by getting close enough to look them in the eyes when you talk to them.

God, I don't want to isolate myself from real people. Help me turn off the distractions and pay attention to people, beginning with looking at them face-to-face.

Big Secret: Tell the Truth

I can't tell you how rare it is to find a truly honest person. Lying and deception are so deeply ingrained into our culture that we think they're okay. Lies may be the norm, but they're never okay.

If you want to become a man of God, learn how to tell the truth. Don't tell half-truths. Don't dodge questions. Speak clearly and answer questions honestly. Fess up when you mess up. Say what you think when asked.

If God knows that you can be trusted to tell the truth in small things, He will trust you to be a man of honor in bigger things.

Jesus never lied, and telling the truth got Him in trouble. It may do the same with you, but it doesn't matter. The truth is always the truth, no matter what you say. So why not tell the truth every time?

I want to be an honest, truthful man
of God. Convict me when I don't tell the
whole truth. Help me speak correctly.

Big Secret: Listen to Grown-Ups

This is not a big secret. Older people are smarter than you. So why do so many young men totally ignore the advice and wisdom of adults?

Don't be a stubborn fool (that's what the book of Proverbs calls someone who refuses to listen to wisdom). Be smart. Ask older people questions about everything you could ever imagine, and note down what they say. Then go do it.

They're smarter than you because they've lived longer than you have. They've already made the mistakes you're going to make, so don't repeat their mistakes when you can avoid them. When a parent or grandparent warns you about the direction you're heading, they have no agenda other than helping you. Listen to them.

I'd give anything if I could ask my parents some more questions, but they're gone. Don't miss out. Listen while you can.

Lord, give me a humble heart and open ears
to listen to the wisdom of those who've gone
before me. Protect me from the mistakes
of a stubborn fool who won't listen.

Big Secret: Treat People Well

Jesus said that we should treat others the way we want to be treated. This is called the Golden Rule. This has been one of my big secrets in life, though it's not a secret at all. It's in the Bible. And wow, Jesus really was right after all!

When you treat people well, you are acknowledging their worth, that they're made in the image of God, and that they have value as people. You're also sowing good seeds that will bear fruit, as those you meet will be more likely to treat others well when they've been treated with kindness.

You're also honoring God by showing kindness to the person He made, and God rewards you for such a good deed. And you never know when someone you've come across in life will be in a place to help you later on in life—and they will remember your kindness to them and return the favor.

Father, remind me that everyone I come
into contact with is Your precious, loved
creation, Lord, and that they need to
be treated with love and respect.

Big Secret: Say No Sometimes

As you get older, the number of opportunities you will have in life will just keep multiplying. Jobs, girlfriends, committees, sports, activities, civic organizations, clubs, you name it. It will never end.

My secret to staying focused is saying no.

You can't do everything just because it's fun or important. You have to eventually pick a job, a wife, a home, and a direction in life. Then you have to say no to everything that would pull you away from those things. Don't worry about hurting people's feelings. They will get over it soon enough.

I'm a husband, daddy, pastor, preacher, and writer. I say no to everything that doesn't serve those purposes, even if I really would love to get involved. The secret is not in doing more things, but in doing a few things well.

Teach me to be focused on who You've called me to be and what You've called me to be, Lord, and to ignore and resist all other opportunities.

MONEY AND STUFF

It All Belongs to God

I hope someone has taught you basic concepts of money and finances, but in case they haven't, I will. The subject of money is mentioned over 800 times in the Bible. It's important—you need to be prepared to handle money, or it will handle you.

The most essential truth is that everything belongs to God. This world, all its treasure and money and nations and empires and armies…it's all God's. That includes your life, your home, your career, your paycheck, and your checking account.

If you begin here, you have a biblical understanding of money. And if you hold money loosely as something God has full access to, you'll manage His money that He loans you as well.

> *God, I believe that all I have is Yours,*
> *especially money. I want to manage it*
> *well, not waste it, and be willing to give it*
> *where and when You tell me to give it.*

Spend Less Than You Make

This should be common sense to people, but it's not. For five years in America—from 2007 to 2012—individuals, families, companies, and our entire government were broke. We'd all gone into debt because we'd all spent more money than we actually had using credit cards and big loans.

Figure out how much money you make each month or each week. Find out how much you spend on food and other bills during that month or that week. And make sure you're spending less than you're bringing in.

Stop buying stupid stuff. Start by cutting out these things—soda, fast food, energy drinks, expensive coffee drinks, excess clothes, music downloads, cable TV, long road trips, and bottled water. Don't buy it if you don't need it.

God, I want my money to reflect my values, and I won't have money to give You if I'm always broke because I spend all my money on things for myself that I don't need. Help me change!

Give to God First

The easiest way to honor God with your finances is to prioritize His kingdom with your money.

The first 10 percent belongs to Him through His church, and beyond that tithe, you get to decide where to invest in the kingdom by giving sacrificially and specifically.

So before you start spending your paycheck on all your bills or yourself, set aside what you've decided to give to God through your church and the ministries you support. That way, you won't forget, and you will be putting God first with your finances in a practical way. When God sees that you're serious about this, He gets serious about giving you more to manage for Him.

You can't outgive God, but it's really fun to try!

Lord, convict me if I ever forget that it's Yours already. I want to put You first, before everything, with my finances. Help me start this simple discipline now.

Save Now, Spend Later

If you want to live like nobody else is living, then you must do what nobody else is doing. You will be the odd man out if you start saving money early in life. But I promise you that it works.

I started saving when I was 10 years old. By the time I was 14, I had over $1000 cash in an old cigar box. Then I opened a checking account. When I started college, I had over $5000 saved up.

I worked hard for every dime of that money. I swept floors, I delivered firewood. I spread hot tar on driveways in the summer. I was more careful with my money because I worked so hard to make it.

Proverbs says that a man gets rich little by little. The goal is not to be rich. The goal is to be generous, and if you learn to save now, you can be generous forever.

Lord, teach me to ignore the selfish voice that
tells me to spend all my money now, and remind
me that generosity starts now, and that saving
allows me to be even more generous in the future.

Practice Generosity

Don't wait until you have a lot of money to be generous. Start right now, right where you are, with the little bit of money you have. Trust me, it's harder to be generous when you have lots of money than when you barely have any. That's why you need to practice generosity before you have wealth. It will become a spiritual discipline that you can carry with you all through life.

I once had a stranger buy me a jacket in the Atlanta airport because I had left mine at home and was going to Indiana where it was freezing cold. I will never forget how God used that stranger to instill in me a desire to be generous on every occasion. I've never gotten over that. You could be that person for someone, so start now in small things.

> *God, give me a generous heart. I want to*
> *start right now practicing the generosity*
> *that You showed me when You rescued me*
> *from the pit of sin and made me Your son.*

Give Systematically

encourage you to pray for God to show you the things He wants you to give to, over and above your local church. Develop a system of giving.

I went to Kenya in my early twenties and God changed my life there, so our family sponsors a little girl in Kenya through Compassion International. My wife and I have traveled to India 11 times and we have a heart for that nation, so we sponsor two children through Hopegivers. We also give every year to a ministry that trains pastors and rescues orphans.

Because I've traveled in 35 countries, I love to support missions agencies that spread the gospel in unreached nations to those who've never heard. This is how I pray and plan our giving. It's not just random. We have a system, but we also give spontaneously when God tells us to.

Lord, I want to develop a plan now, while I'm
young, that will help me be more consistent
and prayerful in my giving. Guide me in
this process and show me where to give.

Give Spontaneously

The more you train yourself to be a generous giver, the more God will give you the desire at random times to give spontaneously, even when you hadn't planned on it.

That's why I keep cash in my wallet, just in case God tells me to give $20 to someone in the store or on the street. Spontaneous giving keeps us fresh, and it keeps our hearts and hands open to God's leading.

Our ministry bought a house once to train young men and women called into ministry, and we borrowed $160,000 to buy the house. Three weeks later, the Lord spoke to a family three states away, and they felt led to pay off the house. We never even made the first monthly payment, because they were obedient when God told them to give spontaneously.

God, I want to be a blessing! Please keep my heart and my hands open so that when You tell me to give, it will be an automatic yes!

Give Sacrificially

A sacrifice is a gift that costs you something. It's not like dropping a $1 bill that you will never really miss anyway in the offering plate. A sacrificial gift is something you can actually feel. I heard a guy say once that it means you've got some skin in the game.

When you think about it, we can't ever really sacrifice anything to God like He sacrificed for us when His Son was crucified and murdered to keep us from having to pay the penalty of our sin. So when we know how much He sacrificed to save us, we are quick to offer up whatever we have to Him, no questions asked, because we know He gave it all for us.

Give up something that you really want so that you can provide something that someone really needs. That's a gift you can feel.

God, I want to offer You my life, my
money, my abilities, my future—all
that I have or ever will have—as a living
sacrifice for Your honor and glory.

IN THE BATTLE

The Battle for Reflection

The Christian life is a battle. If someone tells you it's easy, they're lying to you or they're not a Christian. You may have times in your life where it's easy—but only for a while, before the next battle comes. As long as you're prepared for battle, you're good. Just don't expect a tea party. This is war.

You're going to have to fight for time spent in reflection. Reflection simply means quiet, unhurried time alone spent thinking deeply about your life, your current state, how you're doing with Jesus, and where you want to go.

You're not going to be able to do this without a fight. This world is addicted to noise, movement, activity, and entertainment. Reflection goes against everything this world pushes you toward. But it's in those quiet times of reflection that you will hear the still, small voice of God whisper to your soul.

Help me rebel against the pattern of this world
when I break away from it all, turn off the noise,
and connect with You in quiet reflection. I need
to do this more often, so help me start now.

The Battle for Attention

Whatever catches your eye gets your attention. There are millions of shiny, sparkling things screaming for your attention every second you're awake. They all promise you things you want, like weight loss or easy money or overnight success. All of these voices are liars.

The only person who deserves to hold your undivided attention is Jesus. When you've seen Him, it's impossible to look anywhere else, because His beauty is incomparable and His love is unequaled. When He caught my eye and captured my heart when I was a teenager, it was as if He took my breath away and never gave it back. I'm more fascinated by Him now than I've ever been.

Fight the temptation to get bored with Jesus and venture off to other loves and pursuits. Keep your eyes on Him. Battle to keep your attention on Him and don't give an inch.

Lord, please do whatever You have to do to get and to keep my attention. When I take my eyes off of You, bring me back home to Your presence.

The Battle for Affection

What is the absolute most important thing in the world for a person to do? When Jesus was asked this question, He quoted a verse from the Old Testament that said we must love God with all our heart, soul, mind, and strength. So the greatest thing God wants from us is our love, our affection—our whole hearts.

This is easy to say and hard to do. Anyone can say they love God, but to actually love Him with our actions daily is like a little civil war inside your heart, where half of you loves Jesus but the other half loves yourself and your sin and never even thinks about Him.

Keep fighting that war and don't surrender until He is your greatest love and has all your affection to Himself. The harder you chase after Him, the more you'll desire His love, and the more you will love Him deeply.

Jesus, I want to love You more. I'm so unfaithful at times with my affection and so inconsistent with my heart. I'm sorry for ever putting anything before You. Forgive me.

The Battle for Transformation

This world wants to transform you into a mindless, self-absorbed consumer who treats women like possessions, ignores the poor, eats and drinks too much, and lives for momentary pleasure. Most guys are following that path, and it leads to destruction.

God wants to transform you into a caring, compassionate man who stands up for the defenseless, honors and respects women, obeys authority, and doesn't waste money or possessions, but uses them for the sake of the gospel.

Fight against the world, and fight for the transforming power of God to be unleashed in your life. It's a constant battle that is fought first in the mind, then in the heart, and finally in the choices you make every day. It's the Holy Spirit who transforms you, and He alone can give you victory in this battle.

Change me, God, and make me a brand-new man who runs hard after You every single day. I won't settle for this world and I won't give in to its lies. I give You control. Now, change me!

The Battle for Intercession

Once you get in the habit of making prayer a normal and automatic part of your day, there's another battle to be fought. And I am still fighting this battle after knowing Jesus for many years.

You will tend to pray mostly for yourself at first. This is natural, so don't freak out. But you need to begin praying for other people too. Make a list of the people you know best who need God the most. Then start praying for them every day by name. This is called *intercession*, and it just means praying on behalf of somebody else.

The more you intercede, the more you'll start loving the people you're praying for, and the more your faith will grow as you see God start to answer those prayers you've prayed for others.

I want to be a man of prayer, Lord, and
I need Your help. Bring people to my mind
who need You, and teach me how to pray for
others even before I pray for myself every day.

The Battle for Submission

Submission isn't about losing control. It's about loving Christ.

But you're a guy so this won't be easy. We're not wired to submit. Actually we're wired to want other people to submit to us. Only the Holy Spirit working in your heart can teach you to love Jesus more by giving up control of small and big things in your life to Him.

The more you submit to Him, the more you learn to trust Him with the results. The more you give up to Him, the deeper you begin to love Him. It's a scary thing to lose control—unless you're giving control to Someone you can trust completely because of His perfect love for you. Every act of submission is a small battle between your will and His Spirit. Let His Spirit win.

I admit that it's hard to submit. My will
is stubborn and I'm hardheaded. Teach
me to trust Your love and affection for
me, God, and I will continue submitting
my life to You, one decision at a time.

The Battle for Definition

You're not defined by what happens to you. You're defined by who you belong to.

You've had some bad things happen to you. And if you live in this world, you'll have more. Some of them will be your fault and some of them won't. The question is, will you let the things that happen to you define you as a man?

Instead, define yourself according to who you belong to. You are a child of God. His beloved son. His friend. His creation. Made in His image. You belong to the strongest, smartest, kindest, most powerful force of love imaginable. Fight against the temptation to let outside forces define you. Find your definition in who you belong to—Jesus Christ!

*I will resist all temptations that come my way
today to see myself as a victim of circumstances.
Instead, Jesus, I will see myself as victorious
through Your sacrifice. Change the way I look at
myself by reminding me to look to You to define me.*

WHO IS JESUS TO YOU?

Jesus, Your Savior

Hopefully you've seen a theme develop in this book. The theme is Jesus. He's the source of life, love, forgiveness, and all good things. But who is Jesus to you, as a young man, personally?

See Jesus as your Savior. When He came to earth as a baby born in a barn to a teenage mom in a no-name village in the Middle East, He was on a rescue mission to save humanity and rescue the world from darkness and destruction.

He is the source of your salvation. He pulled you from a burning building. He became your life raft when you were drowning. He was the cure for the cancer of sin. He was the antidote for the poison that ran through your veins. Without Him, you were hopelessly lost. With Him, you're saved and rescued and made new.

Thank You, Jesus, for saving me! Thank You for bearing the curse of sin on my behalf. Thank You for coming to me when I couldn't get to You.

Jesus, Your Lord

The first confession the early church made after Jesus rose from the dead and ascended back to heaven was three simple words: Jesus is Lord.

This confession had serious consequences. It meant that Jesus was superior to all things, people, powers, princes, kingdoms, empires, and kings.

See Jesus as your Lord—your boss, master, ruler, and king. He's not like a political tyrant or a dictator. He rules with love and mercy, and as the absolute sovereign authority over your life, He calls the shots. So remember that His end game is not abusing you like a slave to get what He wants. His agenda is to have a loving relationship with you, to restore you and all of creation to His original design.

I confess that You are Lord and I am not.
You're in control and it's my joy to follow
You and know You and be loved by You.

Jesus, Your Friend

It may seem like a big jump to think of Jesus as your Lord, and then to see Him also as your friend, but He's big enough to be both.

The Bible says that there is a friend who sticks closer than a brother. Jesus is that friend. It also says that Jesus was known as a friend of sinners. So He obviously cares about people.

He's more than a disconnected outer-space deity. He's up close, involved in your life personally—right there when you need Him, like your very best friend you know will be there no matter what. He won't abandon you when you fail. He doesn't bail out when you blow it. He stays with you because He loves you and has invested so much in you already. He's going to stay with you till the end, because that's what a friend does.

Thanks for being a true and trusted friend to me, Jesus. It gives me such peace to know that You're with me no matter what happens. There's no better friend than You.

Jesus, Your Foundation

Everyone builds their life on something. You should build yours on Jesus.

You'll be tempted to build your life on some other foundation—money, education, popularity, success, accomplishments, fame, or pleasure. But none of these things is strong enough to support the weight of your life. However, Jesus is strong enough. Build your life on Him.

If a foundation is shallow or weak, the house will eventually crumble and fall. If the foundation is firm, solid, and deep, the house stands strong. When you build your life on the person and the completed work of Jesus, you weather the storms, you withstand the trials, and you stand firm for the glory of God.

Jesus, You're my foundation. I choose to build my life on You, to base my identity in what You've done for me, and to settle all questions I'll ever have by the truth of Your Word.

Jesus, Your Protector

The world we live in is obsessed with safety and security, and for good reason. School shootings, terrorist attacks, and the threat of nuclear war have created a paranoid culture, with metal detectors and law enforcement personnel on every corner.

Ultimately, however, nothing and no one can protect you but Jesus. He's more powerful than any threat, and His authority is unlimited. He's with you, He's in you, and He's for you.

So look at Jesus as your protector. Nothing will happen to you that He doesn't know about or allow, and anything that happens to you under His providence, though it may seem bad, will eventually be used for good. He bought you with His blood, and you belong to Him. He takes care of His own.

Jesus, I rest in Your protection. I feel peace knowing that You're sovereign over all things, and You watch over me with Your loving-kindness.

Jesus, Your Treasure

I want you to learn this as a young man—the ultimate goal of a Christian is not to one day go to heaven. The ultimate goal is to one day get Jesus.

The thing that makes heaven awesome is that Jesus will be there. Jesus is your treasure.

Streets of gold will be cool, but really, would you be happy in a place like heaven if Jesus weren't there? No! It wouldn't be heaven without Him.

My dream is to one day hear Jesus say to me, "Well done! You were a good and faithful servant to me, and I'm glad you're here. Let's spend eternity together." That's the goal. Jesus Himself is the treasure worth finding, and He is worth living for today.

When I forget why I'm here or what I'm living for, remind me that it's You, Jesus. You're far better than any phony treasure this world could offer me. You're real, and You're forever!

Jesus, Your Everything

Life makes no sense without Jesus. Suffering, pain, loss, death, tragedy, and grief affect everyone. If you don't know Jesus, there's no hope and no reason and no ultimate purpose in anything. Everything is just random and meaningless.

But if you belong to Jesus, He is the answer for all questions, the purpose behind all of life, the source of all hope and joy, and the motivation for getting out of bed every morning. Only in the death and resurrection of Jesus for the salvation of the world can you make any sense out of everything that's ever happened in human history and everything that's happened, and will happen, to you.

God had a plan from the beginning, and His plan was Jesus. He is everything, and in Him, all things are made new. Including you.

*You're my everything! Nothing in this world
saves me or satisfies me but You, Jesus. I long to
see You face-to-face and be with You. I can't even
imagine how awesome and perfect You really are.*

A Word from Clayton About Crossroads Worldwide...

I n 1995, I began a nonprofit ministry out of my college dorm room called Crossroads.

It began with my preaching ministry and now includes multiple layers of ministry that stretch all around the world.

- *Summer camps.* Several thousand middle- and high-school students come from all over the United States every summer to our Crossroads summer camps, where they hear teaching and preaching from God's Word and participate in group activities, sports tournaments, corporate worship, and community missions.

- *Student conferences.* Every January during Martin Luther King Jr. weekend, we host a three-day conference for middle- and high-school students, as well as a separate conference for college students and young adults.

- *Mission trips.* We send short-term volunteer teams to India, Malaysia, Haiti, the Navajo reservation in Arizona, and various other places to share the gospel. We also support a full-time volunteer couple in the Himalayas as they assist in running a Christian hospital.

- *Community discipleship home.* We host two intensive discipleship programs for people ages 18 to

25, one in Boiling Springs, North Carolina (a 12-month program), and one in Manali, North India (a 6-month program).

- *Preaching ministry.* I travel full-time, teaching and preaching on evangelism, discipleship, missions, and relationships. I speak at conferences, colleges, churches, retreats, concerts, and public schools. I began this ministry at age 14 and have preached in 45 states and 30 countries to over 2 million people.

- *Writing.* In addition to the six books I have written, I consistently write about issues that face Christians, pastors, leaders, parents, and spouses on my blog at www.claytonking.com.

- *Media.* I have hundreds of audio and video sermons online for free. Find them at
  www.claytonking.com
  www.newspring.cc
  www.liberty.edu
  iTunes: "clayton king live"
      or "clayton king"

For more information or to schedule one of our speakers, contact us at
www.crossroadsworldwide.com
crossroadsworldwide@gmail.com
704-434-2920

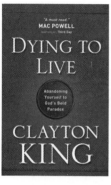

Dying to Live

Abandoning Yourself to
God's Bold Paradox

Do you want to *live*? Do you want to be sold out to something that will outlive you and outlast your existence? Then you have to die. It's the only way to gain life. The only way to fill that deep-inside longing. The only way to really know Christ—because it's *His* way.

Clayton King shares 20 bold pictures from Scripture, his own life, and the lives of others that will

- make you sick of existing just to get more stuff, money, and "success"
- grip your soul with longing for the life Jesus promised
- stir up your passion for God's mission to build a kingdom that will last forever

It's a reality that's no longer about you.

"You wake up to a world filled with colors and tastes and textures and conversation and songs and laughter, a world that no longer revolves around your own petty drama but around God's bigger story of rebuilding what we have all broken."

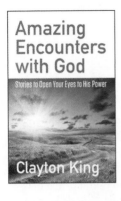

Amazing Encounters with God
Stories to Open Your Eyes to His Power

Where do you want to meet God today?

Clayton King points to real-life experiences that show how God speaks through the everyday occurrences of life. At any moment, He is there, giving you the chance to open your eyes to Him—as happens when Clayton…

- has an enlightening conversation with a drunken millionaire on an airplane
- witnesses a miracle of biblical proportions in a small Himalayan village
- plans what he thinks will be a quick down-and-back hike to the bottom of the Grand Canyon
- considers a horse sticking its head through a barbed-wire fence
- has a surprise encounter with the IRS

These compelling, thought-provoking stories will encourage you that God is always at work in your life, even in the very ordinary. And when He breaks in with the unexpected—which happens about a trillion times a day in our world—you can step back, pause for a moment, and gaze in awe and admiration.